More than Humanitarianism: A Strategic U.S. Approach Toward Africa

D1005118

More than Humanitarianism: A Strategic U.S. Approach Toward Africa

Report of an
Independent Task Force

Sponsored by the Council on Foreign Relations

Founded in 1921, the Council on Foreign Relations is an independent, national membership organization and a nonpartisan center for scholars dedicated to producing and disseminating ideas so that individual and corporate members, as well as policymakers, journalists, students, and interested citizens in the United States and other countries, can better understand the world and the foreign policy choices facing the United States and other governments. The Council does this by convening meetings; conducting a wide-ranging Studies program; publishing *Foreign Affairs*, the preeminent journal covering international affairs and U.S. foreign policy; maintaining a diverse membership; sponsoring Independent Task Forces; and providing up-to-date information about the world and U.S. foreign policy on the Council's website, www.cfr.org.

THE COUNCIL TAKES NO INSTITUTIONAL POSITION ON POLICY ISSUES AND HAS NO AFFILIATION WITH THE U.S. GOVERNMENT. ALL STATEMENTS OF FACT AND EXPRESSIONS OF OPINION CONTAINED IN ITS PUBLICATIONS ARE THE SOLE RESPONSIBILITY OF THE AUTHOR OR AUTHORS.

The Council will sponsor an Independent Task Force when (1) an issue of current and critical importance to U.S. foreign policy arises, and (2) it seems that a group diverse in backgrounds and perspectives may, nonetheless, be able to reach a meaningful consensus on a policy through private and nonpartisan deliberations. Typically, a Task Force meets between two and five times over a brief period to ensure the relevance of its work.

Upon reaching a conclusion, a Task Force issues a report, and the Council publishes its text and posts it on the Council website. Task Force reports reflect a strong and meaningful policy consensus, with Task Force members endorsing the general policy thrust and judgments reached by the group, though not necessarily every finding and recommendation. Task Force members who join the consensus may submit additional or dissenting views, which are included in the final report. "Chairman's Reports" are signed by Task Force chairs only and are usually preceded or followed by full Task Force reports. Upon reaching a conclusion, a Task Force may also ask individuals who were not members of the Task Force to associate themselves with the Task Force report to enhance its impact. All Task Force reports "benchmark" their findings against current administration policy in order to make explicit areas of agreement and disagreement. The Task Force is solely responsible for its report. The Council takes no institutional position.

For further information about the Council or this Task Force, please write to the Council on Foreign Relations, 58 East 68th Street, New York, NY 10021, or call the Communications office at 212-434-9679. Visit our website at www.cfr.org.

Task Force Chairs

(signature)

Anthony Lake

(signature)

Christine Todd Whitman

Project Directors

(signature)

Princeton N. Lyman

(signature)

J. Stephen Morrison

Task Force Members

J. Dennis Bonney

Lael Brainard

Chester A. Crocker*

Alex de Waal

Nicholas Eberstadt*

Richard Furman

Helene D. Gayle

Victoria K. Holt

Gregory G. Johnson

Richard A. Joseph

Anthony Lake

Nicholas P. Lapham*

Rick A. Lazio

Princeton N. Lyman

J. Stephen Morrison

Michael E. O'Hanlon*

Raymond C. Offenheiser

Samantha Power

John H. Ricard

Gayle E. Smith

Christine Todd Whitman

*The individual has endorsed the report and submitted an additional or a dissenting view.

Working Group Members

Anthony J. Carroll
Manchester Trade Ltd.

Timothy Docking
*Millennium Challenge
Corporation*

Laurie J. Fitz-Pegado
The Livingston Group

Christopher Fomunyoh
*National Democratic Institute for
International Affairs*

Tom Gibbian
Emerging Markets Partnership

Stephen Hayes
The Corporate Council on Africa

Makila James
Department of State

Jeffrey R. Krilla
International Republican Institute

Marina S. Ottaway
*Carnegie Endowment for
International Peace*

Dave Peterson
*National Endowment for
Democracy*

Carol Pineau

Witney W. Schneidman
*Schneidman & Associates
International*

Joseph T. Siegle
*Center for Institutional Reform
and the Informal Sector*

Note: Working Group members participate in their individual and not institutional capacities.

Contents

Foreword

This was the "year of Africa." Africa figured prominently at world summits. Rock stars staged concerts to focus public attention on the continent. The industrialized democracies pledged to double aid to Africa and forgive the debt of fourteen of the continent's poorest countries.

Attention and commitments, though, are not the same as results. For this reason, the Council on Foreign Relations established an Independent Task Force to examine whether the United States was getting Africa policy right.

Africa is of growing international importance. By the end of the decade, for example, sub-Saharan Africa is likely to become as important a source of U.S. energy imports as the Middle East. China, India, Europe, and others are competing with each other and with the United States for access to oil, natural gas, and other natural resources. The world's major powers are also becoming more active in seeking out investments, winning contracts, and building political support on the continent.

Africa is also one of the battlegrounds in the fight against terrorism. Osama bin Laden based his operations in Sudan before setting up shop in Afghanistan. Terrorists struck U.S. embassies in Africa years before the 9/11 attacks. Africans are actively recruited for terrorist operations in South Asia and the Middle East, including Iraq.

Mass killings in the Darfur region of Sudan and the persistence of conflict on the continent challenge the world's will to spotlight, prevent, and stop atrocities. Africa is also the epicenter of the world's most serious health pandemic, HIV/AIDS.

The Task Force evaluated U.S. Africa policy in light of Africa's growing importance. The Task Force's main finding is that U.S. policy toward Africa should change to reflect Africa's growing strategic importance. Washington should maintain its historic and principled humanitarian concerns, while broadening the basis for U.S. engagement on the continent. The Task Force also recommends that the United States advance a policy to help "integrate Africa more fully into the global economy," so that the advantages of globalization no longer bypass the continent.

I am grateful to two outstanding public servants, Anthony Lake and Christine Todd Whitman, for agreeing to chair this Task Force. They brought political insight, intellectual leadership, and a wealth of experience to a critical but often neglected set of issues. I would also like to thank the Task Force members, who came to this effort from many different backgrounds, for the purpose of advancing the shared interests of the United States and Africa. Project Directors Princeton N. Lyman, the Ralph Bunche senior fellow for Africa Policy Studies at the Council on Foreign Relations, and J. Stephen Morrison, director of the Africa Program at the Center for Strategic and International Studies (CSIS), did a tremendous job in bringing the many issues and recommendations together into this report. I am grateful to them, as I am to the entire Task Force.

Richard N. Haass
President
Council on Foreign Relations
December 2005

Acknowledgments

The Council was fortunate to have two distinguished Americans as chairs for this Task Force, Anthony Lake and Christine Todd Whitman, who brought broad experience and strong leadership to the work. They recognized the growing importance of Africa to the United States and emphasized the need for this report to speak of that importance not only to policymakers but to the American public.

We also thank the members of the Task Force, who brought a wide variety of skills and knowledge to our deliberations. Throughout the past year, in meetings, written input, and many e-mail exchanges, they contributed to every aspect of the analysis, findings, and recommendations. Special thanks are also due to individual Task Force members who provided venues for previewing the report with business, philanthropic, and civic organizations, and for organizing two dynamic working groups on the promotion of private investment and the improvement of governance and institutions in Africa.

The Africa Advisory Board for the Council's Africa Studies program provided the original inspiration and guidance for the establishment of the Task Force. Members of the committee later reviewed the draft report and provided other insights. Special thanks go to the board's chairman, Vincent Mai, and its members: Franklin Thomas, Frank Ferrari, Kenneth Bacon, Kofi Appenteng, Walter Kansteiner, Peggy Dulany, Bryan Hehir, Gay McDougall, Alan Patricof, Antranig Sarkissian, Frank Savage, and Carl Ware.

The Task Force benefited significantly from the contributions made by Task Force observers and working group participants, who provided additional expertise and important input. The Task Force is also grateful to several persons outside the Task Force who contributed to the agenda and agreed to review the report at various stages. These included three members of the Council's International Advisory Board: Khehla Shubane, Mark Chona, and Baba Gana Kingibe and Council member Frank G. Wisner. Also contributing in this regard were Professor Ephraim Isaac; Kenneth F. Hackett, executive director of Catholic Relief Services; and Jennifer Cooke, codirector of the CSIS Africa Program.

Council President Richard N. Haass gave strong support and encouragement for the creation of the Task Force, read drafts, and provided valuable recommendations for the report's presentation and argumentation. The Task Force program's Executive Director Lee Feinstein and Assistant Director Lindsay Workman, provided guidance throughout the Task Force process. Lee read numerous drafts, reviewed outreach plans, and recommended valuable changes to the structure of and recommendations in the report. Lindsay did yeoman's work to provide much needed guidance and support throughout the process. Council staff members Lisa Shields, Irina Faskianos, and Anya Schmemann worked closely with us to develop an extremely active outreach program. And the Council's publications team, Patricia Dorff and Molly Graham, were essential in putting this report in its final form.

We express our deepest appreciation to Cheryl Igiri, the Task Force's research associate, for her tireless commitment to this project. And the Task Force could not have succeeded without the administrative support from Council on Foreign Relations interns Sayo Abayomi and Jeff Cary.

We are also deeply indebted to the CSIS Africa Program staff for their substantial and generous contribution in personnel and support throughout the life of this project. Special thanks are due to CSIS Research Associates Kelley Hampton and Nelly Swilla.

Finally, the Task Force and the Council appreciate the Ford Foundation's generous financial support, which made this project possible. We are ever grateful to Susan Berresford and Michael Edwards for their encouragement.

Princeton N. Lyman and *J. Stephen Morrison*
Project Directors

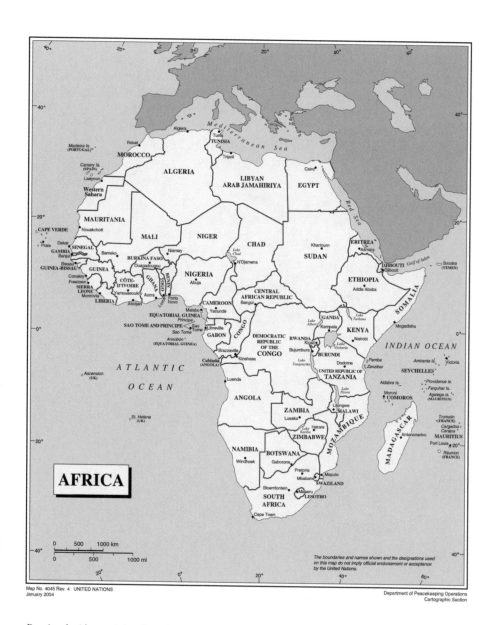

Reprinted with permission from the UN Cartographic Section, Map No. 4045 Rev. 4, January 2004.

Acronyms

ABC	Abstinence, Be faithful, use Condoms
ACOTA	Africa Contingency Operations Training and Assistance
ACRI	African Crisis Response Initiative
AGOA	African Growth and Opportunity Act
ANC	African National Congress
APRM	African Peer Review Mechanism
ART	antiretroviral treatment
ASEAN	Association of South East Asian Nations
AU	African Union
CACF	China-Africa Cooperation Forum
CENTCOM	U.S. Central Command
CIA	Central Intelligence Agency
CJTF	Combined Joint Task Force
CNPC	China National Petroleum Corporation
COMESA	Common Market of Eastern and Southern Africa
DDR	Disarmament, Demobilization, and Reintegration
DFID	UK Department for International Development
DRC	Democratic Republic of the Congo
ECOWAS	Economic Community of West African States
EITI	Extractive Industries Transparency Initiative
EPA	Environmental Protection Agency

EU	European Union
EUCOM	U.S. European Command
EX-IM Bank	Export-Import Bank
FDLR	Democratic Forces for the Liberation of Rwanda
FY	fiscal year
G8	Group of Eight
GMO	genetically modified organism
GPOI	Global Peace Operations Initiative
GSPC	Salafist Group for Preaching and Combat
HIPC	Heavily Indebted Poor Countries Initiative
HIV/AIDS	Human Immune Virus/Acquired Immune Deficiency Syndrome
ICC	International Criminal Court
IFPRI	International Food Policy Research Institute
IMF	International Monetary Fund
IMO	International Maritime Organization
LIFE	Leadership and Investment in Fighting an Epidemic
LRA	Lord's Resistance Army
MCA	Millennium Challenge Account
MDGs	Millennium Development Goals
MFA	Multifiber Agreement
NAS	National Academies of Sciences
NATO	North Atlantic Treaty Organization
NDI	National Democratic Institute for International Affairs
NEPAD	New Partnership for Africa's Development
NGO	nongovernmental organization
NSC	National Security Council
OAS	Organization of American States
OECD	Organization for Economic Cooperation and Development
OGAC	Office of the Global AIDS Coordinator
OPIC	Overseas Private Investment Corporation
PAGAD	People Against Gangsterism and Drugs
PEPFAR	President's Emergency Plan for AIDS Relief
PSI	Pan Sahel Initiative
SADC	Southern African Development Community

SME	small and medium-sized enterprise
SOCOM	U.S. Special Operations Command
SPLM	Sudan People's Liberation Movement
TSCTI	Trans-Sahara Counterterrorism Initiative
UNAIDS	United Nations Programme on HIV/AIDS
UNIDO	United Nations Industrial Development Organization
UNITA	National Union for the Total Independence of Angola
USAID	U.S. Agency for International Development
USTDA	United States Trade and Development Agency
WTO	World Trade Organization

Task Force Report

Introduction

The Council on Foreign Relations organized the Independent Task Force on U.S. Policy toward Africa because it is important for Americans to recognize that Africa has become of steadily greater importance to the United States and to global interests. The timing was fortuitous because in 2005 Africa rose to the top of the global agenda. Africa was the principle topic when the leaders of some of the world's most powerful nations, the Group of Eight (G8), met in Gleneagles, Scotland, in July. A week earlier, Africa's poverty was the focus of worldwide concerts witnessed by two billion people.

Yet, the focus of these events on Africa's humanitarian needs, as vital and rewarding as such attention was, largely overlooked other critical ways in which Africa is important to the United States. The Task Force set about examining these other linkages to U.S. foreign policy objectives and the components of a more comprehensive U.S. policy toward Africa. It concluded that a more comprehensive policy toward Africa is needed. The Task Force also believes that such a policy will better address Africa's humanitarian needs by helping to bring about related policy changes and a more effective use of resources to hasten the continent's integration into the global economy and the prospects for long-term economic growth.

The report deals primarily with sub-Saharan Africa. This is a somewhat artificial distinction. Egypt, Libya, Algeria, Tunisia, and Morocco all play important roles on the continent; and, except for Morocco, all of the North African countries are members of the African Union

(AU) and participants in its activities. But this distinction between North and sub-Saharan Africa follows that of the Department of State and recognizes that North Africa looks as much to the Middle East as it does southward. Development analyses also tend to single out sub-Saharan Africa because of the prevalence of poverty and a number of shared ecological, political, and economic concerns. Nevertheless, in the discussion of terrorism and of conflict resolution, the report calls attention to the interplay of northern and sub-Saharan Africa, and the need for the U.S. government to develop better cross-bureau coordination on these issues.

The Task Force brought experts on Africa together with a broad representation of religious leaders, humanitarians, human rights advocates, business leaders, and security experts. The Task Force met three times in the spring of 2005 and continued to review analyses of individual topics and policy, as well as drafts of the final report throughout the summer and fall. In addition, the Task Force consulted with African leaders, other humanitarian experts, and U.S. government officials.

The report is divided into four main sections. The first chapter presents the findings and recommendations of the Task Force. This is followed by more in-depth analyses of four issues that the Task Force found to be of new and increasing importance in Africa's relation to the United States: energy, competition from China and other countries, terrorism, and the growing impact of Human Immune Virus/Acquired Immune Deficiency Syndrome (HIV/AIDS). The report then examines the more traditional and familiar components of U.S. policy in Africa and how they can be better addressed in the context of a more comprehensive policy: conflict resolution and peacekeeping, democracy and human rights, and economic growth. The final, concluding chapter draws the themes of the report together and summarizes the steps forward.

2005 Was the Year for Africa, But We Missed the Point

In June 2005, two billion people around the world viewed the "Live 8" concerts, headed by famous rock musicians Bono and Bob Geldof, which passionately appealed for an end to poverty in Africa. A week later the leaders of eight leading industrial nations pledged to double aid to Africa, forgive the debts of fourteen of Africa's poorest countries, and bring life-saving drugs to all individuals suffering from AIDS by 2010. President George W. Bush joined in this dramatic moment, outlining how the United States would, along with others, double its aid to Africa. These were noble commitments that reflected deep humanitarian impulses. They responded to real needs in one of the world's poorest regions.

But the point that was missing—amid the music, the communiqués, and the commitments—is that Africa is becoming steadily more central to the United States and to the rest of the world in ways that transcend humanitarian interests. Africa now plays an increasingly significant role in supplying energy, preventing the spread of terrorism, and halting the devastation of HIV/AIDS. Africa's growing importance is reflected in the intensifying competition with China and other countries for both access to African resources and influence in this region. No less important, these events did not speak to how Africa continues to test the resolve of the international community and the United States to prevent mass killings and genocide, as the continuing atrocities in the Darfur region of Sudan most clearly demonstrate.

These public events also reinforced an outdated view of Africa. Not a single African leader, teacher, doctor, or nurse was featured on the Live 8 stages. Africa's leaders in all walks of life are not passive objects but active players with influence over the dynamics in their region. A core of democratically elected presidents is leading the continent in the direction of greater democracy, improved governance, and sound economic policies. Civil society workers, officials, and business people are working to improve their countries at all levels of African life. This rising level of African leadership—some 40 percent of African states are electoral democracies—offers an opportunity to build strong partnerships in areas of mutual interest.

The Task Force finds that Africa is of growing strategic importance to the United States in addition to being an important humanitarian concern. In a world where economic opportunity, security threats, disease, and even support for democracy transcend borders, a policy based on humanitarian concerns alone serves neither U.S. interests, nor those of Africa. Furthermore, the Task Force Report finds that critical humanitarian interests would be better served by a more comprehensive U.S. approach toward Africa. In sum, it is not valid to treat Africa more as an object of charity than as a diverse continent with partners the United States can work with to advance shared objectives.

Current U.S. Policy

There has been a steady increase in attention to Africa in both the Clinton and Bush administrations. Each president made at least one high-profile visit to the continent, each has frequently spoken publicly about Africa, and each harnessed bipartisan congressional support since the mid-1990s for steady increases in assistance and support of U.S. programs to mitigate violent conflicts.

The Bush administration launched two new assistance programs, the Millennium Challenge Account (MCA) and the President's Emergency Plan for AIDS Relief (PEPFAR), which direct significant amounts of new resources to Africa. These two programs figure prominently in President Bush's pledge to double U.S. aid to Africa by 2010. The African Growth and Opportunity Act (AGOA) opened up more of the U.S. market to African countries as the result of a bipartisan initiative within the Congress in 2000. AGOA was welcomed and enhanced by the Clinton administration, and since that time has been supported and elaborated by the Bush administration. President Bush has made a strong commitment to eliminating subsidies and other barriers to Africa's agricultural exports, if other countries, most importantly members of the European Union (EU), do the same. Several antiterrorism programs have been initiated since 9/11, including stationing 1,200–1,800 U.S. and allied troops in Djibouti, patrolling Africa's east coast, assisting countries in tracking terrorists in the Sahel region of West Africa, and helping several countries in East Africa to enhance their intelligence capacities. The wealthy G8 member countries have agreed to a U.S. proposal to train up to 40,000 African peacekeepers to help implement negotiated peace settlements. Secretary of State Condoleezza Rice has specifically included Africa in the U.S. priority focus on enhancing democracy around the world and has singled out Zimbabwe for special attention. The Bush administration has given sustained high-level attention to resolving the civil war in Sudan, helping to establish a more legitimate broad-based government there, and addressing the vast humanitarian toll and continued threat of mass atrocities, including genocide, in Sudan's Darfur region.

At the same time, the public rhetoric surrounding Africa policy has continued to emphasize humanitarian concerns more than other multiple and rising U.S. stakes. Recent increases in U.S. aid to Africa have been primarily in emergency assistance, with long-term investments in growth essentially flat. Congress, moreover, has not followed through on earlier pledges of assistance, most recently cutting back on the president's request for the MCA. While democracy has been stated as a major objective, there are very limited funds for Africa within worldwide democracy programs, and no articulated strategy to address the major challenges to democracy that loom in the influential states of Ethiopia, Nigeria, and Uganda, or the tyranny in Zimbabwe that was singled out by Secretary Rice. Antiterrorism programs have been primarily military in nature without adequate political oversight or complementary political, public diplomacy, or economic programs. Nothing similar to the high-level attention given to Sudan has been devoted to other major conflicts that threaten the stability and economic development of major subregions, such as the civil war in the Democratic Republic of Congo (DRC), and the threat of renewed war between Ethiopia and Eritrea, where the United States had played a significant role in resolving the earlier fighting. And Darfur begs for still greater U.S. action to mobilize international support in order to secure the ground and compel a negotiated settlement.

The United States has yet to make a geopolitical shift to pay sufficient attention to West Africa's energy rich Gulf of Guinea, where billions of dollars are changing hands with impact that is both positive and negative. U.S. policy has not responded to the implications of intensifying activity in Africa by China along with other Asian countries. This activity may have consequences not only for access to resources but perhaps more importantly for the pursuit of important U.S. objectives of good governance, protection of human rights, and sound economic policies.

Consequences of Continuing Down the Same Path

A broader basis for U.S. policy toward Africa is a more sustainable one for engagement with Africa. Recent assistance and humanitarian initiatives will likely suffer without a more comprehensive elaboration of U.S. interests in Africa, both to Congress and the public. A better understanding of the challenges in Africa, as well as the positive changes taking place in African leadership, good governance, sound economic policies, and cooperation with the United States on terrorism, democracy, and trade, will bolster confidence in a deeper U.S.-Africa relationship. The consequences of not doing so are becoming apparent. Growing domestic concern over deficits and the growing cost of natural disasters, as well as the war in Iraq, is already beginning to put pressure on foreign assistance funds. Congress has reduced the president's fiscal year (FY) 2006 request for the MCA by more than half, putting into jeopardy the president's pledge to double aid to Africa by 2010. The United States has begun to pressure the United Nations to cut back on its peacekeeping operations in West Africa, largely as a cost-saving measure, even though the peace processes in that subregion are still quite fragile. Aside from assistance, eliminating U.S. subsidies and trade protection for American agricultural producers is vital to integrating

Africa more fully into the global economy. Such a move will be politically difficult and must be justified on both national security as well as humanitarian grounds to overcome strong domestic opposition.

The United States must thus recognize and act on its rising national interests on the continent through a far higher mobilization of leadership and focused resources that target Africa's new realities. A business-as-usual approach will squander historic opportunities to change the course of Africa's development and advance U.S. interests. Africa's poverty will persist. Conflicts and instability will likely continue to trouble many countries. The ability of Africa to resist terrorist infiltration and extremist appeals will be weak; stability and corruption in the energy-producing states will be a cause for public concern, as well as a threat to predictable production; and U.S. influence will decline. Quite remarkably, U.S.-Africa policy still retains a strong bipartisan base of support in Congress and enjoys a widening and deepening support within American society. A more robust and comprehensive policy is therefore within reach.

We will know that the response to this opportunity has failed, however, if in another ten years, U.S. policymakers link hands once again with other world leaders around Africa's problems and the world witnesses another global concert to end Africa's poverty. The United States cannot afford to let another decade go by without effective solutions, and Africa deserves far better.

What is New?

AFRICA IS BECOMING MORE STRATEGICALLY IMPORTANT

Energy. Africa is becoming more important because of its growing role in supplying the world with oil, gas, and non-fuel minerals. Now supplying the United States with 15 percent of oil imports, Africa's production may double in the next decade, and its capacity for natural gas exports will grow even more. In the next decade, Africa could be supplying the United States with as much energy as the Middle East.

The United States is facing intense competition for energy and other natural resources in Africa. China, India, Malaysia, North Korea, and South Korea are all becoming active in the search for these resources and for both economic and political influence on the continent.

European countries and Brazil are stepping up their aid and investments as well.

China presents a particularly important challenge to U.S. interests and values. China does not share U.S. concern for issues of governance, human rights, or economic policy. For example, China combines its large stake in Sudan's oil industry with protection of the government of Sudan from UN sanctions for the ongoing attacks in Darfur.

Terrorism. Africa is becoming more important in the war on terrorism. Terrorist cells struck U.S. embassies in Kenya and Tanzania in 1998. Terrorist organizations more recently have sought refuge in West Africa's Sahel region. Africans are being recruited for terrorism in Iraq and have been implicated in the subway bombings in London.

Disease. Africa is more important today because it is the epicenter of the HIV/AIDS pandemic, which is rapidly reaching the stage where it will not only take a steadily rising death toll but will also undermine social and political stability as well as the prospects for economic progress on the continent. What the United States learns in Africa, and what it is able to achieve, will be critical to whether it is possible to stem this pandemic as it spreads across Asia and into Russia.

Global Cooperation. African states are beginning to cooperate on the global stage. For example, African nations, with nearly a third of the votes in the World Trade Organization (WTO), are in a position to provide critical support to the United States in the current world trade negotiations. At the same time, African countries, together with other developing nations, are challenging the United States and Europe to make major changes in agricultural trade practices that would enable Africa to build its export capacity and become better integrated into the world economy.

Stopping and Preventing Genocide. In Darfur, the world is once again being tested as to its readiness and willingness to halt acts of genocide and crimes against humanity. Two years into the Darfur crisis, the situation remains unresolved despite strong U.S. and other denunciations of these acts and the introduction of African peacekeepers. Over two million displaced persons continue to suffer from periodic attacks and the breakdown of humanitarian operations.

African Governance and Capacities are Improving

Many African leaders have strengthened their commitment to constitutional rule, improved economic policy, good governance, and conflict resolution. While there is a long ways to go before these commitments are fulfilled across the continent, several concrete steps have been taken to achieve them.

Africa has dispatched its own peacekeepers to almost all of the countries in conflict. Africans need outside assistance to maintain these deployments and to bring about an end to the most serious conflicts. However, they are prepared to act with external support and additional capacity.

Africa's most influential and capable countries (e.g., South Africa, Nigeria, Kenya, Ghana, and Senegal) are providing important leadership. Burundi is a good example, where genocide on the scale of Rwanda could have taken place. Determined South African leadership in mediating a new political consensus and the readiness of the AU to deploy peacekeepers quickly, ahead of UN forces, combine to enable the United States, Europe, and the UN to play important supportive roles, but without anywhere near as much high-level involvement and investment of resources as needed in Sudan.

Bipartisan Support for Africa is Growing in the United States

Aid levels to Africa have been rising steadily since the mid 1990s, through Democratic and Republican administrations, and with bipartisan support in Congress. President Bush pledged to double aid to Africa again by 2010. AGOA, a major opening of the U.S. market to African exporters, was fashioned with bipartisan congressional support during the Clinton administration, and has been steadily expanded during the Bush administration.

The United States brought the HIV/AIDS issue to the UN Security Council in January 2000—the first time a health issue was recognized as a threat to international peace and security. In 2003, President Bush galvanized international support for addressing this pandemic with a dramatic pledge of $15 billion over five years.

Since the late 1990s, the United States has supported a steadily increased UN peacekeeping presence to contain conflicts in Africa. President Bush and the other members of the G8 have pledged under the Global Peace Operations Initiative (GPOI) to support the training of 40,000 African peacekeepers over the next five years.

In addition, the public constituency for Africa is broadening. Joining a long tradition of support for Africa from the African-American community, humanitarian organizations, and select members of Congress, an increasing number of religious groups have become engaged in African issues. Evangelical Christian groups played a leading role in galvanizing U.S. leadership in resolving Sudan's decades-long civil war. They have been active in raising public awareness of the atrocities in Darfur. Evangelical and other religious groups have become principal advocates for debt relief for poor African countries and in the fight against HIV/AIDS.

Student groups are taking up African issues. A coalition of college students created the "Save Darfur" campaign, advocating stronger U.S. action on the Darfur situation, and lobbying for divestment in the China National Petroleum Corporation (CNPC).

U.S. military commands in Europe and the Middle East have recognized the strategic role of Africa, with an emphasis on the terrorist threat in Africa and the security of energy installations. This sharply contrasts with the traditional Pentagon view that Africa has little strategic importance.

The rapidly increasing programs to combat HIV/AIDS have enlisted interest and involvement from public health schools and professional organizations, along with rising numbers of nongovernmental organizations (NGOs).

Positive Movement But Significant Challenges

U.S. policy has begun to respond to new realities and opportunities, but the policy is fragmented and geared more toward short-term emergencies than to long-term investments.

As noted above, the United States launched several valuable foreign assistance initiatives that are international in scope but focus particularly on Africa, such as the MCA that was scheduled to increase U.S. foreign aid worldwide by 50 percent by 2007; PEPFAR; the major trade initiative, AGOA; and a $1.2 billion malaria initiative. New programs for counterterrorism, such as the Combined Joint Task Force in Djibouti and the Trans-Sahara Counterterrorism Initiative (TSCTI), were launched after 9/11.

Nevertheless, the slow start of the MCA and Congress's decision to cut the president's request for 2006 in half call into question the prospect for doubling aid to Africa by 2010. Almost all of the five-fold increase in U.S. aid to Africa over the past ten years has been in emergency aid, rather than in the long-term investments that could lift Africa out of poverty. Investment in Africa's agricultural development declined sharply during the 1990s, higher education programs were largely terminated in the same period, and infrastructure projects continue to be rare. Even with new initiatives aimed at humanitarian need (e.g., educational exchanges and safe drinking water), Africa often loses out to regions considered to be of greater strategic importance. President Bush's clean water initiative in FY 2000 earmarked only $1.4 million for Africa out of an $80 million program, with the balance going to Afghanistan and the Middle East.

Support for HIV/AIDS programs, which grew substantially after President Bush's $15 billion initiative, has begun to slip. At the last meeting of the Global Fund to Fight AIDS, Tuberculosis, and Malaria (hereafter the Global Fund), only half the required funds for the coming year were pledged.

U.S. diplomatic presence in several of the energy-producing and other critically important countries is minimal. There is no ambassadorial presence in Khartoum; no American diplomatic presence in northern Nigeria, home to Africa's largest Muslim population, which exceeds 60 million persons; and none along the Mombasa coast in Kenya, where terrorist cells persist. Political oversight of the counterterrorist programs is insufficient. The Pan Sahel Initiative (PSI) worked with two regimes, Mauritania and Chad, without sufficient U.S. attention to either country's poor human rights and governance records.

The direction of U.S.-Africa policy and programs is fragmented. There are three separately administered major foreign assistance programs operating in Africa. Antiterrorist programs are being directed by three separate military commands. The National Security Council (NSC) has not taken sufficient lead on global energy issues in a way that would focus attention on Africa's growing role and the attendant challenges it creates. Peacekeeping programs are underbudgeted and divided between separate bureaus and departments.

Shaping a More Comprehensive Africa Policy

The guiding premise of this report is that Africa is of strategic as well as humanitarian importance to the United States. The long-standing emphasis on humanitarian interest outside this broader context serves neither African nor U.S. interests today. Failure to broaden the basis for U.S. policy will make it exceedingly difficult, in the face of growing budget pressures in the United States, to maintain and deepen promising commitments for development, HIV/AIDS, and security initiated in the past several years. The recent congressional cutback of MCA funding and shortfalls in support of UN peacekeeping are harbingers of this danger.

The Task Force believes it is critical to develop a new, comprehensive U.S. policy toward Africa that maintains the historic and principled concern for humanitarian issues, while broadening the basis for U.S. engagement. Such a comprehensive policy should place Africa squarely in the mainstream of U.S. global policy objectives. The Task Force recommends that the United States advance a policy to help integrate Africa more fully into the global economy. The new policy would also mean making Africa an active partner in U.S. programs to assure safe and reliable supplies of energy for the world market, combat terrorism, reduce conflict, control pandemic diseases, and enlarge the worldwide community of democracies.

This is a big agenda. Africa policy is made even more challenging by the fact there are forty-eight countries in sub-Saharan Africa with quite different circumstances, influence, and potential. At the same time, many of the most challenging problems, such as disease, conflict, and terrorist activity, extend across borders, demanding both bilateral and regional responses. Sometimes the most disturbing crises occur in countries not thought of as strategically important. Rwanda in 1994 was such a case, where the crisis and the ensuing genocide touched the most basic values of the American people.

But the growing African capacity and willingness to lead on many of these issues, the bipartisan support that can be mobilized for a more comprehensive policy, and the partners with whom the United States can share responsibility make this challenge manageable. Several of these policy objectives are also mutually reinforcing. Integrating Africa more fully into the global economy, and helping various states to overcome conflict, will strengthen African states and their societies' resistance to extremism and terrorism. Better use of oil and gas proceeds will enhance stability and increase the ability of influential states like Nigeria and Angola to contribute to peace, growth, and stability throughout the continent. Moreover, the alternative to a comprehensive policy is to go along, as in the past, with admirable but insufficient programs, with the high probability that Africa will remain outside the mainstream of the world economy, still poor and heavily dependent upon aid, and still vulnerable to instability and future crises with possible genocidal dimensions. All the new and vital U.S. interests in Africa would suffer. The United States can do much better, and must, for its own sake. The Task Force has identified the following priorities and goals as integral to a comprehensive Africa policy.

Integrate Africa into the Global Economy. Trade reform is one of the most critical priorities if Africa is to grow and become more fully integrated into the global economy. The G8 leaders' pledge to double aid is welcome and can be used to bolster Africa's economic and social condition. But this commitment alone will not fully integrate Africa into the global economy or reduce aid dependency by the end of the next decade. It will not address the fundamental problems of poverty or conflict that wrack the continent today.

Together with adequate technical assistance and trade reform within Africa, the elimination of U.S. and European barriers to Africa's agricultural exports could add hundreds of millions of dollars annually to

African earnings, reduce substantially rural poverty, and place many countries on the path to self-sufficiency. The United States should follow through on the president's commitment at the UN to eliminate all tariff and subsidy barriers in agricultural trade if other nations do so, by urging all the members of the WTO to set firm timetables for going down this path. The current Doha trade round is the crucial period for doing this, and the opportunity should not be lost.

Reform and Prioritize U.S. Assistance. In doubling aid, consistent long-term commitments of nonemergency assistance are needed. The United States should fulfill the president's pledge at the 2005 G8 Summit to double U.S. aid to Africa by 2010, but with an emphasis on aid for long-term investments in growth and development, not counting emergency aid that may be necessary during that time period.

Increases in aid should give consistent attention, not just for five but for ten to twenty years, to development areas where the United States has special strength and that address some of Africa's most important needs: agricultural development; private sector facilitation; science and technology; HIV/AIDS, malaria, and children's health needs; education; population; a sustainable environment; and—in support of all of these—democratization.

These programs should all emphasize building and supporting African leadership, institutions, and expertise, involving African governments, civil society, the New Partnership for Africa's Development (NEPAD), and the AU. Democracy is making progress across Africa, but the United States needs to focus especially on influential states where the democratic process is under stress. Special attention should thus be paid over the next two years to supporting constitutionally based political transitions and electoral processes in Nigeria, Sudan, Uganda, and Ethiopia. Success in those countries will reinforce the AU's ability to promote democracy more broadly. The United States should also help build AU institutions for enforcing human rights. To combat deeply ingrained patterns of corruption, which are major obstacles to development and democracy, the United States and European countries should provide strong support to African anticorruption efforts through assistance to civil society, advocacy organizations, and through help in both criminal investigations and recovery of illegally obtained assets.

Population programs must be restored to their earlier priority. Ideological issues and shifting of attention to HIV/AIDS have led to a diminution of U.S. leadership in this area. Yet the demographic projections in Africa should give the United States serious concern. Famine-prone countries like Ethiopia and Niger have doubled their population in the past two decades and the projections suggest further sharp increases in the future. In particular, the social and political impact of the growing youth bulge should garner more attention to population policy, as this bulge presages more conflict, unemployment, and potential recruitment for extremist activity.

The United States needs to urge the World Bank to develop a more coordinated strategy for overall donor assistance to Africa that will reduce overlap, assure consistent attention to all key sectors, and relieve some of the administrative problems burdening developing countries. Presidential and congressional leadership is required to reduce the heavy U.S. reliance on its own procedures, the many "earmarks" in the aid legislation that limit U.S. flexibility, and the resistance to allowing other donors to lead and coordinate policies in various sectors. The United States should support greatly expanding the UN emergency reserve fund of both food and funding so that recurring natural calamities such as drought do not turn into full-blown famines, which then demand the highest level of U.S. policy attention and massive emergency responses.

Confront the True Scale and Complexity of the HIV/AIDS Pandemic. Strong presidential leadership, well beyond this administration, will be needed to fulfill not only the $15 billion commitment under PEPFAR but the even greater amount of resources needed in the decades ahead. The commitment by the G8 in 2005 to see that all those in need worldwide have access to treatment represents an enormous commitment to future funding that has yet to be calculated. The United Nations Programme on HIV/AIDS (UNAIDS), however, projects a 50 percent increase in requirements in just the next four years.

The United States must mobilize other donors to commit to a rising level of support for HIV/AIDS programs as the pandemic reaches major proportions across the continent. In particular, the United States must press other countries to meet two-thirds of the required budget for the Global Fund. Congress has limited the U.S. contribution to one-third of what is pledged.

Other donors should also be urged to fund the broader health infrastructure needed in Africa to complement the U.S. focus on emergency programs and HIV/AIDS-specific delivery systems. Donors, host governments, and the private sector need to come together to develop new, more appropriate models for delivery of health services in the poorer and most affected countries. The shortage of skilled health workers and infrastructure, aggravated by the recruitment of African doctors and nurses by developed countries, is one of the major limiting factors in delivering HIV/AIDS programs as well as addressing Africa's other critical health needs.

Along with other donors and African countries, the United States must give greater attention to prevention, or else the pandemic will constantly run ahead of the international community's ability to bring it under control. Ideological differences must be set aside and support given to all those prevention programs that work, including Abstinence, Be faithful, use Condoms (ABC). Much more research is needed on how to change social behavior, including gender dynamics, and more African leadership needs to be mobilized behind that objective. New approaches must be developed to increase testing, as the vast majority of those believed to be infected do not know they have the virus and are thus not accessible for counseling or treatment.

Promote a Reliable Supply of Energy from Africa. A geopolitical shift is needed in U.S. energy policy. The United States should establish a U.S.-Africa energy forum, at the cabinet or sub-cabinet level, to promote regional cooperation and to discuss shared problems of security, transparency, and marketing. The United States should upgrade its diplomatic presence in energy-producing countries, especially in the Niger Delta region, Equatorial Guinea, and São Tomé and Príncipe. Cabinet level visits to energy-producing states should be undertaken more often.

Nigeria, Angola, Chad, Equatorial Guinea, São Tomé and Príncipe, Gabon, and Cameroon will soon be joined by Mauritania, and perhaps

Namibia and South Africa, as well as states along Africa's east coast, as energy producers. Oil and gas can provide much needed earnings for these countries to address the needs of their people. But oil has too often been a curse, leading to corruption, waste, environmental degradation, decline of the non-energy sectors of the economy, and unrest. A reliable and responsible policy for assuring the supply of energy from these states therefore requires not only investment in production facilities, which the private sector will do, but encouraging responsible use of oil and gas proceeds by the producing states. Few of these states will qualify for the MCA or traditional forms of aid. The United States should therefore utilize other sources of aid (e.g., the Economic Support Fund) to provide training, education, democratization programs, and security assistance, and to develop public-private partnerships to build infrastructure. Strong support should be given to civil society groups to advocate for greater transparency by the government in the use of energy proceeds and for better investment in development, environmental protection, and job creation for people in oil producing areas.

Military assistance should be provided to help states in the Gulf of Guinea improve security of coastal environments and develop regional maritime security programs. Security assistance and intelligence sharing should be provided to combat the large-scale theft of oil, arms trafficking, and money laundering that fuel violent instability in the Niger Delta region. A recently announced program between the United States and Nigeria for this purpose is a positive development.

Build Security Against Failed States and Other Sources of Terrorism. The president has already indicated that failing states are potential breeding grounds for terrorism. Africa, however, does not receive sufficient political attention on the threat or sufficient funding to combat it.

The Department of State should exert more political oversight of counterterrorism programs to avoid collusion or unintended support of repressive regimes, as happened in Mauritania. Special attention must be paid to human rights concerns, the misuse of the terrorist label to punish legitimate opposition, and the use of the military for oppression of ethnic or religious groups.

The United States needs to rebuild its intelligence capabilities in Africa to understand better the dimensions of the threat, the sources of unrest, the warning signs of collapse, and the most appropriate forms of U.S. response, whether economic, cultural, political, or military. Nigeria and Somalia are examples of where such intelligence is badly needed.

More funding for Africa should be added to the president's Transitional Initiative for fragile and post-conflict states. Currently, $275 million out of a total of $325 million are designated for four countries: Afghanistan, Ethiopia, Haiti, and Sudan. This leaves insufficient funding for fragile countries in Africa such as the DRC, Liberia, Sierra Leone, Angola, Burundi, Rwanda, and the Central African Republic. The Transitional Initiative can fund democratization, civil society, civil security, and conflict resolution programs, all of which are essential in these states.

The administration has proposed for FY 2006 an expanded program of education and exchanges for countries with significant Muslim populations. But only the trans-Sahel region of Africa is mentioned, though this program would be valuable in many other African countries as well.

The U.S. Agency for International Development (USAID) should reverse the 1995 decision to close its missions in Niger, Chad, and other African states that are now important to the war on terrorism. These are the very states where U.S. European Command (EUCOM) is providing military assistance, but where broader development programs would be equally, if not more, important.

Roaming bands of former militia and child soldiers pose a specific threat to stability and are a ripe source of recruitment for rebels and terrorist groups. Peacekeeping budgets need to be expanded to cover the costs of Disarmament, Demobilization, and Reintegration (DDR) programs for ex-combatants in post-conflict countries. Currently these programs are inadequately funded through sundry bilateral and multilateral sources and, when funded, the financing often arrives too late to achieve the successful integration of ex-combatants. Liberia, Sierra Leone, and the DRC are prime examples of where more funding is urgently needed.

Dedicate High-Level Leadership to Reducing Conflict. High-level attention from the White House and senior officials in the Department of State must be given to resolving major conflicts in Africa, especially those that threaten whole subregions or involve large-scale atrocities. Africans have taken a strong leadership position in bringing conflicts to an end, but they often lack the political influence, the resources, and the peacekeeping capacity to do it alone. The success of U.S. interventions can be seen from their use in bringing an end to the Ethiopia-Eritrea war in 2000 and, most recently, the civil war in Sudan.

Such attention should be now devoted to the DRC, where some four million people have died, civil strife continues, and the peace process is extremely precarious. Two other targets for such attention are the continuing tension between Ethiopia and Eritrea, where U.S. counterterrorism interests are affected; and the still fragile peace processes in Liberia and Sierra Leone. A return to conflict in either country could engulf the whole West Africa subregion. Budgeting and funding of UN peacekeeping need reform. The administration's budget requests to Congress do not take into account even known new peacekeeping operations, let alone allow for rapid support in fast-breaking crises. For example, full U.S. funding is not yet available for the anticipated UN mission to Sudan, which may be one of the largest ever, and which may have to be expanded further to address the crisis in Darfur. Recently, the United States opposed the UN secretary-general's request for an expansion of the UN peacekeeping force in the DRC in advance of elections there, as well as the extension of the full UN peacekeeping mission in Liberia past March 2006, largely for budgetary reasons. In both the DRC and Liberia, the U.S. position risks weakening the peace process. Such reasoning also undermines effective peacekeeping and efforts to meet UN mandates with adequate capacities.

The budgets and policy direction for U.S. bilateral support for African peacekeeping also need reform. They are divided among several programs, departments, and bureaus to a degree that makes both long-term planning and the assessment of the total resources being devoted to this objective difficult. Policy direction should be consolidated at a sufficiently high level in the Department of State, and plans made for both short- and long-term programs. For example, the president's commitment under the GPOI to train up to 40,000 African peacekeepers over five years is a major positive step. But funding requests beyond

FY 2005, when funding was obtained from the Department of Defense, do not provide sufficient funds to keep this program on track. It is also not clear how the needed increases in funding for the crisis in Darfur will affect GPOI's funding or from what source such funding will be found at all.

Prevent Future Atrocities. Failure to prevent the genocide in Rwanda was a major moral failure for the international community. The loss of life was horrific. It was also a political failure, lowering the credibility of the international community's readiness to live up to its commitments under the Convention on the Prevention and Punishment of the Crime of Genocide and the promises of "Never Again." The genocide also touched off the instability and warfare that has engulfed Central Africa ever since.

Nevertheless, the ongoing fighting in Darfur represents another deeply disturbing instance of genocidal acts and crimes against humanity. President Bush wrote "Not on my watch," when he read of the earlier Rwanda debacle. As a result, the United States condemned the killings in Darfur as genocide, urging strong UN actions against the government of Sudan and, along with the EU, assisting the deployment of an African peacekeeping force. Currently, Deputy Secretary of State Robert Zoellick is devoting his personal attention to the issue and has assigned Roger Winter, special envoy for Darfur, to help resolve this crisis and work on the other aspects of peace in Sudan. Yet, two years and as many as 100,000 deaths later, the international response remains woeful. More than two million people remain displaced from their homes, subject to periodic attack, and without sufficient protection by either AU or other peacekeepers. Meanwhile the government of Sudan, the sponsor of the acts that the United States and the UN have condemned, remains free of serious sanctions.

The United States must press for urgent international action. First, the AU must be convinced that, despite its efforts to do so, it is not capable of mobilizing and deploying the full 13,000 peacekeepers it has promised. The AU is concerned about losing credibility if it seeks outside help in deployment and command. But it risks an even worse loss of credibility if the situation continues to deteriorate. The AU should request that the UN authorize a coalition of willing countries to provide a protective force, including some from Africa, for the internally displaced persons within Sudan. This coalition could serve as a bridging force to UN "blue helmets" (i.e., UN soldiers). The need is urgent and only a non-UN coalition could deploy rapidly enough to meet the current need. The force should have a mandate to defend the population against further attacks and to take military action, as necessary, to counter the threat. This includes enforcing the no-fly zone against the government of Sudan. An AU request would moreover serve to override previous Sudanese objections to a non-African force.

The UN Security Council remains blocked by the Chinese and Russians from imposing strong sanctions against the government of Sudan. The United States and its European partners should begin to impose further sanctions of their own on companies doing business in Sudan and on arms shipments to Sudan, and should even consider ways to inhibit Sudanese oil exports. China should be put on notice that continued blocking of UN sanctions is a serious issue for the United States, and that U.S. and European sanctions are in the works. China should be made aware that this issue could well provoke a serious confrontation between China and the United States.

The rebel forces continue to be part of the problem. Now splintered and without a clearly defined political agenda, they are poorly equipped to participate in the negotiations to end the conflict hosted by the AU. Rebel forces are increasingly guilty of attacking aid workers and stealing humanitarian supplies. The United States, together with interested European countries, must continue to engage the rebels on these matters, as Deputy Secretary Zoellick began doing in Nairobi, and provide technical assistance to them for political negotiations. The United States must also take a strong position against further attacks on humanitarian missions. The United States should make great efforts with Eritrea, Chad, and factions in southern Sudan, to cease material support to the rebels and to help guide the rebels to a more constructive negotiating position.

The United States should press southern Sudanese leaders, now members of the central government, to take a much more active role in stopping government attacks in Darfur. Southern attention to Darfur has declined with the death of former Sudan People's Liberation Movement (SPLM) leader John Garang. The United States should condition the delivery of the large amounts of aid pledged to southern Sudan on active southern involvement in achieving a negotiated settlement in Darfur.

The Darfur crisis is part of a larger situation in Sudan in which the Khartoum government has failed to share power and resources with outlying regions. Both northern and southern members of the government of Sudan should be put on notice that, without broadening representation in the government and sharing resources with marginalized areas of the country like Darfur and eastern Sudan, the United States will not provide the full political or economic support promised under the Comprehensive Peace Agreement, signed in January 2005, which ended the north-south civil war.

Beyond Darfur. Neither the United States nor the UN has developed an adequate system for preventing or even containing such calamities in the future. Article 8 of the Genocide Convention, an injunction to prevent genocide, is the most important responsibility in the convention, much more so than acting after genocide has happened.

The United States should actively seek agreement that the UN secretary-general be charged with bringing to the attention of the Security Council evidence of impending large-scale atrocities, whether or not to be formally labeled as genocide, as clear threats to international peace and security. The new UN special adviser on the prevention of genocide, now a part-time post with a limited mandate, should be charged with, at the early stage of such crises, assembling reports of mass killings or impending disasters from official and non-official sources; convening as necessary those with field knowledge; evaluating the evidence; and reporting to the secretary-general on the need for bringing the matter urgently to the Security Council.

As with Darfur, the United States and its allies must be ready to take appropriate action, including sanctions and, if necessary, military intervention, if the Security Council is blocked from doing so.

Answer China's Challenge. The United States has to recognize that there is a new playing field in Africa that requires new resources and more active diplomacy. To compete more effectively with China, the United States must provide more encouragement and support to well-performing African states, develop innovative means for U.S. companies to compete, give high-level attention to Africa, and engage China on those practices that conflict with U.S. interests. Specifically:

- The MCA should begin to provide dramatically higher levels of assistance to African states performing well in governance, human rights, and development policies, in contrast to China's assistance packages that ignore these criteria. Congress must be persuaded to fully fund the projected increases for the MCA, with half of MCA's funding going to Africa.

- Presidential and other high-level visits are important and should include a presidential visit to the AU, where emphasis can be placed on its support for good governance and sound development policies.

- The United States should develop public-private partnerships, utilizing the Export-Import Bank (EX-IM Bank), the Overseas Private Investment Corporation (OPIC), and USAID, in combinations that would enable the United States and U.S. companies to participate and compete more effectively for infrastructure and other projects needed in Africa.

- The United States should engage China on "rules of the road" in Africa, to end support for egregious violators of human rights, reduce incentives for corruption, protect the environment, improve the long-term prospects for stability, and reduce unfair business practices. Deputy Secretary Zoellick's broaching with China its protection of "rogue states," in September 2005, and Assistant Secretary of State for African Affairs Jendayi E. Frazer's discussions in China later in the year, are good steps in this direction.

- The United States should also look to cooperate with China in Africa on programs where both countries are active, especially health and peacekeeping.

Improve Policy Direction and Coordination. Implementing a complex and multifaceted policy requires high-level attention along with the necessary multiplicity of program instruments. At present, the programmatic instruments are not sufficiently led and coordinated to achieve maximum impact, nor do they constitute a balanced application of political, economic, and security assets.

There are various ways in which the government might be strengthened to provide more coordinated policy direction and to assure that there is sustained support for multiyear funding for development and security programs, and trade reform. This could be done through one or more of the following: a stronger NSC role in chairing an Africa policy committee, the creation of new high-level positions to coordinate critical parts of the policy (e.g., energy, post-conflict stabilization and reconstruction, and joint military command structures), or by elevating the responsibilities and staff resources of the Department of State specifically charged with Africa policy. The Task Force does not recommend any one of these over another, but urges the U.S. government to give high priority to improving coordination through these or other means.

The United States should appoint a fully accredited ambassador to the AU. The United States has taken this step with nearly every other regional organization (e.g., the North Atlantic Treaty Organization [NATO], the Organization of American States [OAS], the Association of South East Asian Nations [ASEAN], and the EU) to the considerable benefit of U.S. foreign policy interests. Such an appointment, if given adequate authority and staff support, will help ensure consistency in the U.S. approach, signal the seriousness of U.S. purpose, and allow a single focal point for U.S. engagement on both immediate priorities and long-term challenges facing the AU. Also, it will provide additional valuable oversight of the multiple streams of U.S. assistance to the AU.

The several congressional committees that address African issues must be partners in the development and oversight of a new Africa policy. These committees will need to provide consistent, long-term support to both the development and security programs discussed in this report. The plethora of earmarks and restrictive conditions that are present in most aid legislation should be reduced, or at least consolidated, in ways that are consistent with the broad and comprehensive approach to Africa that this report recommends. Congress should also provide the executive branch with a peacekeeping emergency reserve that would allow the administration, with appropriate consultation with

Congress, to respond rapidly to new or expanding demands in conflict situations.

Trade reform will demand exceptional and far-sighted leadership in Congress. Hearings on Africa, including those on security interests and on the role Africa plays in the overall trade negotiations important to the United States, should help in garnering support for ways to reduce U.S. agricultural support programs and tariffs with appropriate adjustment assistance to affected farm communities.

A Unique Opportunity

This "year of Africa" provides an exceptional opportunity to turn all the attention, and the added resources that may flow from it, into a far more comprehensive and effective policy toward Africa. It could lead to a deeper understanding of U.S. interests in Africa and to a more comprehensive and productive long-term policy. Or it could be but a superficial, passing phase for U.S. policy, a feel-good era of promises, in which the United States fails to grasp the deeper shifts that are occurring and fails to graduate to a more coherent, strategic approach to Africa, backed by adequate human and financial resources.

The newer, broader approach this report advocates requires high-level leadership—the voices of the president, the secretary of state, and others—articulating a new integrated vision of how to advance U.S. interests in Africa. The vision must encompass Africa's growing importance to the United States—in energy, security, global health, and trade. It must impart to the American people a sense of commitment to addressing U.S. interests more effectively, including embarking upon a long-term commitment to helping achieve a fundamental improvement in Africa's place in the world. The vision must recognize the changing playing field in which the West's interests are being challenged, especially by a strongly competitive China and other fast-growing economies in Asia. This vision must make clear the diversity of Africa and the positive changes taking place that make wisely planned, increased investment there much more likely to be successful.

With this vision, the year of Africa can be a turning point; not a passing phase, but rather the beginning of a serious long-term commitment to achieving the United States' and Africa's best interests.

The Expanding Energy Sector

Africa, and in particular West Africa, holds steadily increasing significance for future U.S. energy supplies. High levels of exploration and production investment in Nigeria and Angola, along with significant growth in other countries along West Africa's Gulf of Guinea, have transformed the region into a strategic supplier of crude oil, and prospectively also of natural gas, to the U.S. and global energy markets. Petroleum development is not confined to the Gulf of Guinea. Both Chad and Sudan are crude oil producers, and exploration is commencing in Ethiopia and off the shores of Kenya and Namibia.

It is increasingly in the U.S. interest to locate new oil sources outside the Middle East. Furthermore, West Africa's sweet, low-sulfur oil has advantages from an environmental standpoint and is easily transported to the eastern U.S. seaboard. The region's current sixty billion barrels of proven reserves may appear small compared to some of the Middle East oil giants, but the global energy market is such that rising mid-range producers like Nigeria and Angola today are increasingly critical to the reliability of supply and stability in global oil prices. Investment by foreign companies in the Gulf of Guinea energy sector is already substantial—$50 billion in this decade. This figure is likely to grow considerably over the next decade as new offshore discoveries of oil are brought into production, generating two to three million barrels per day in new crude oil production, and as West Africa becomes a new major global exporter of natural gas.

However, in contrast to the world's other fast-growth, offshore energy zones—Brazil, the Caspian, the U.S. Gulf of Mexico—the volatile mix of factors seen in the Gulf of Guinea is striking and exceptional. Its acute vulnerability to instability and disruption stems from corruption, weak governmental structures, limited regional integration (especially in the maritime sphere), the presence of large criminal syndicates based in Nigeria, organized mercenary groups able to project themselves from South Africa and into the Gulf of Guinea, the threat of armed insurgency in Nigeria's Niger Delta, the possibility of radical Islamist action rooted in northern Nigeria or the Sahel, and the potential instability of several autocratic governments.

In the past, petroleum operations in West Africa have weathered instability and turmoil. Oil imports continued to flow even during the worst excesses of the military regime of Nigeria's Sani Abacha and through Angola's three decades of bloody civil war. But the nature and context of U.S. engagement in Africa have changed fundamentally, and commercial investment in the oil sector operates in an environment where powerful nongovernmental groups, focused on human rights, transparency, and environmental management, command the attention of shareholders, the media, policymakers, and members of Congress. The United States today has multiple pressing interests: promoting democratic processes, actively promoting growth and reliable petroleum supplies from Africa, combating HIV/AIDS, and curbing global terror.

In this new context, the United States cannot successfully pursue its multiple interests in the Gulf of Guinea through vertical or compartmentalized policies. U.S. engagement with West Africa's energy sector needs to be undertaken through a broad, multilateral approach that balances energy security with democratic governance and transparency, internal stability, equity, environmental stewardship, development, and diversification of energy supply.

U.S. Energy Interests

U.S. energy security is based on achieving a stable supply of energy at affordable prices from as diverse a set of suppliers as possible. In a global oil market that has seen demand surge and prices reach as high as $70 per barrel, expansion of production in the Gulf of Guinea is a positive development.

It has been projected that one in five new barrels of oil that enter the global market between 2005 and 2010 will come from the Gulf of Guinea, potentially raising its contribution to U.S. imports from 15 percent to over 20 percent. The region will enjoy over $33 billion in onshore and offshore capital investment from 2005 to 2010. More than 40 percent of this increase is projected to come from U.S.-based companies. New oil will come overwhelmingly from deepwater production in Nigeria, Angola, and Equatorial Guinea. The region's importance to the United States is due not only to the scale of U.S. investment, its share of U.S. imports, and the U.S. citizens who help explore and produce those volumes, but also to the fact that the Gulf of Guinea countries produce low-sulfur, sweet crude oil that is highly valued by the U.S. market.

The region is quickly assuming a global importance with respect to natural gas. The United States is expected to rely increasingly on imported natural gas to fuel the increasing demand for power generation as its own domestic supplies mature and begin to decline. Nigeria, Equatorial Guinea, and Angola are each constructing major liquefied natural gas export infrastructures that will place West Africa in a prominent competitive position worldwide later in this decade.

Major Threats to the Gulf of Guinea's Viability

CRIMINAL NETWORKS

Perhaps the most immediate threat to U.S. interests in Africa's oil-producing states emanates from the Niger Delta region, where organized crime syndicates operate a major crude oil theft operation with alleged partners in regional refineries. Well-armed and increasingly well-financed militias back these criminal networks. And the militias have begun to operate with greater autonomy and skillfully exploit ethnic and economic grievances to muster popular support. Estimates of the level of this theft range from 70,000 to 300,000 barrels per day. With current prices in the $60 per barrel range, even the low estimate of 70,000 would generate over $1.5 billion per year—ample resources to fund arms trafficking, buy political influence, or both.

The Nigerian government has taken several significant actions to curb the oil theft problem, seizing some ninety-five vessels and arresting several senior and mid-ranking naval officials. In a May 2005 visit with President Bush, Nigerian President Olusegun Obasanjo explicitly asked the United States for assistance in curbing money laundering, arms trafficking, and illegal oil sales. The United States and Nigeria announced an agreement along these lines in December 2005.

But the progress to date also reveals troubling aspects of the problem. The prosecutions confirm suspicions that oil theft activity infiltrates the highest echelons of the Nigerian navy and possibly similarly ranked officials in other parts of the Nigerian government. Enforcement has been mixed. There is also awareness that while oil theft has armed and politicized the Niger Delta, it has also generated significant cash wealth that has been used by authorities at the federal and state levels to keep the Delta under political control.

While Nigeria seems to be taking oil theft more seriously, it is hampered by a lack of technical capacity and the absence of an effective political strategy. U.S. naval experts estimate that Nigeria could put in place the necessary surveillance equipment and training to detect oil theft, intercept offenders, track vessels, and maintain security in their ports for a cost of $100 million. Nigeria and other countries, which are likely recipients of stolen crude oil for their refineries, do not share intelligence in a way that would facilitate interception. There is clearly room for security assistance to combat oil theft and to facilitate training for a regional interdiction capability. In addition, the United States has deep experience with international coordination and assistance to combat money laundering and other financial crimes. A U.S. pilot program for interdiction and to curb piracy might test Nigeria's resolve and demonstrate the effectiveness of a coordinated interdiction program.

Terror

The threat of terrorist attacks in West Africa against U.S. or Western interests is real, although assessments vary widely on the precise level and nature of the threat. Terrorist action in Nigeria would have deeply destabilizing effects on oil production. In 2004, threats against foreign oil workers by self-styled Nigerian Delta warlord Alhaji Dokubo-Asari drove world oil prices skyward. Asari, who has used popular grievance together with massive revenues from stolen oil to build his support base, illustrates the disruptive power that rhetoric and threats alone can wield. Though Asari is currently under arrest, his supporters are threatening further violence if he is sentenced harshly.

Concern over Islamist-inspired terrorist threats focuses principally on Nigeria's northern region. Some analysts fear that indigenous groups, supported by radical Islamist groups following Osama Bin Laden's exhortation in early 2003 to focus on Nigeria, might seek to exploit rising discontent with the government in Abuja and its close ties with the West, and possibly make largely Western-owned oil infrastructure a soft target for attack.

Political Instability

Prolonged political instability in any of Africa's oil producers could damage U.S. oil interests. U.S. engagement to address the threat of instability will require an expanded and more robust diplomatic presence in each of the target countries.

NIGERIA

Nigeria is a nascent democracy. Among its challenges are internal ethnic and economic divisions, notably a dangerous polarity between the Muslim-majority north and a largely Christian south. Corruption, organized crime, and uneven governmental administrative capacity leave the country open to potential exploitation by indigenous radical Islamist groups, possibly in league with outside partners, intent on discrediting or damaging the current government and its external ties. Unrest persists in the southern Niger Delta states, where onshore production is concentrated. Local leaders complain of years of underdevelopment, extreme poverty, and unrealized expectations. The suppression of dissent in the Delta, together with armed violence and the existence of armed militias, makes for a potentially explosive combination. State governments, which enjoy significant revenues from federal revenue sharing and the complementary efforts of the Nigeria Delta Development Corporation, have shown little capacity to distribute these monies fairly or effectively.

Nigeria has begun a promising, but preliminary, program of economic reform to bring transparency to its fiscal management, including the management of its energy sector, and to root out public corruption. These initiatives raise high public expectations and face deeply entrenched vested interests. They also remain vulnerable to potential political reversals. Nigeria will need additional assistance to carry out its reform program, to design and implement effective programs to curb money laundering, to further procurement reform, to audit its public enterprises, and to root out the causes of crude oil theft.

ANGOLA

Since the end of the Angolan civil war, building cooperation and consensus between the victorious government and a debilitated National Union for the Total Liberation of Angola (UNITA) has proven slow and difficult. Talks over constitutional reform, electoral laws, and oversight arrangements are proceeding slowly. At present, elections are slated for 2006, though a precise date has not yet been set. Failure to hold elections in 2006, after repeated earlier delays, would cast a shadow over the government's stated commitment to the democratic process. When national elections do occur, it is likely a full fifteen years will have passed since the first (and only other) democratic election in Angola's tortured history.

Internally, the climate within Angola has improved somewhat. Independent Angolan monitoring groups are able to function, the judiciary has been used less frequently to repress and intimidate dissent, and Protestant and Catholic clergy have become far more active in lobbying for reconstruction, accountability, respect of human rights, and attention to easing the abject poverty of most Angolans.

Reform in the management of Angola's oil wealth is centered, as it has been for years, on Angola's dialogue with the International Monetary Fund (IMF). That dialogue is prone to dramatic swings, and is focused on bringing about preliminary reforms prior to the introduction of an IMF staff monitoring arrangement. But recent developments have given Angola additional financial flexibility and room for maneuver. The entry of the Chinese, who agreed in 2004 to a $2 billion low-interest, long-term facility for reconstruction, coupled with high oil prices, has made reaching an agreement with the IMF more difficult. The United States currently derives 4 percent of its oil imports from Angola. That number could double in the next five years.

SMALLER STATES

Promoting enduring democratic reform and stability in Equatorial Guinea, Gabon, São Tomé and Príncipe, Cameroon, and Chad is no less difficult.

The Nguema family has ruled Equatorial Guinea, a country of 535,000 people, since independence in 1968. President Teodoro Obiang Nguema Mbasogo survived an externally financed coup attempt in 2004, which appears to have been engineered by a group of South African mercenaries. There have been reports of continued coup plotting in 2005 involving mercenaries recruited out of the Niger Delta. Equatorial Guinea has risen in a short time to be West Africa's third largest crude oil exporter. With nearly $5 billion invested to date, ExxonMobil, Amerada Hess Corporation, and Marathon Oil are major U.S. investors. This amount may double over the next five years. The country remains vulnerable to external coups due to its lack of defense capability, such as police, coast guard, or military. The United States has criticized the Equatorial Guinea government for human rights violations, failure to invest in social spending, and person trafficking. Sustained U.S. efforts will be needed to encourage an open political space, now largely absent, for nongovernmental groups to operate.

In São Tomé and Príncipe, there is a fledgling democratic system with a record of tolerance, but it remains highly fragile and prone to periodic breakdown. Government capacity, for all its intentions, is remarkably thin. Its oil sector and overall national governing system operates very much in the shadow of Nigerian influence. Beginning in 2003, popular anticipation of future oil wealth, fueled by the first bidding round and signing bonuses for the offshore blocks managed jointly with Nigeria, intensified interparty rivalry and tensions, triggering a mercenary-led mutiny and coup attempt that was reversed following intervention by President Obasanjo and others. Since that time, the country has passed through successive internal upheavals. It is unknown how much offshore oil wealth São Tomé possesses: estimates vary between four and ten billion barrels. The country will remain a choice target for adventurers, and the management of wealth streams will remain a formidable internal challenge.

In Chad, the newly completed Chad-Cameroon pipeline scheme provides the basis for an important Revenue Management Program. This program is a partnership that joins the Chadian government, NGOs, the World Bank, and major oil company investors to provide oversight for the disbursal of oil revenues, and earmarks monies for education and health. Crude oil began flowing in 2004, and thus far this scheme has functioned reasonably well. Nonetheless, Chad remains fundamentally unstable; its autocratic government resists pressures for democratic reform and is vulnerable to recurrent coup plotting within the security services. Continued strife along its border area with the Darfur region of Sudan has also aggravated instability within the Chadian government. A sign of trouble is the Chadian President Idris Deby's recent proposal to divert more of the oil proceeds to security and less to social investments.

Addressing the Threats

In recent years, a number of promising regional initiatives have arisen, some of which could help build regional capacities and foster a greater sense of collective regional responsibility to eliminate potentially destabilizing threats. Already, for example, the Gulf of Guinea states have peacefully resolved a number of contentious maritime and land boundary disputes. Furthermore, new global attention to the challenges of improving governance, promoting transparency and accountability, and encouraging reform offers opportunities to work collaboratively with African states and European partners to avert some of the destabilizing tendencies—exacerbated in some instances by rapidly increasing oil revenue—that have plagued the region in previous decades.

The Gulf of Guinea Commission is a regional organization conceived by President Obasanjo in 1999 and founded by member states Nigeria, Angola, Gabon, Equatorial Guinea, the Republic of Congo, and Cameroon. Its intended purpose is to promote economic cooperation in the region; provide a framework to monitor and control environmental degradation and harmonize exploitation of natural resources (including petroleum and fisheries); and coordinate common positions related to peace and stability in the region. The commission has the potential to serve as a mechanism to prevent and mediate conflicts arising in the region. To date, only two states, Nigeria and São Tomé, have ratified the treaty to formalize the organization. For this forum to be successful, the fears of member states that the commission will be a Nigeria-controlled endeavor will need to be resolved.

The International Maritime Organization (IMO) has recently forged an alliance to provide technical assistance to over twenty Gulf of Guinea ports in order to promote compliance with the International Ship and Port Facility Security Code. This code is a systematic risk management mechanism to help detect and deter security threats, and collect and share security information in maritime areas. This new alliance could be an important first step in improving surveillance and response capacity to check oil theft, piracy, and illegal fishing.

In 2003 EUCOM proposed the Gulf of Guinea Guard assistance and training program to improve control of coastal areas, enhance physical security of national ports, and promote cooperative maritime security. In October of 2004, EUCOM assembled Gulf of Guinea Chiefs of Naval Operations, who had never before met as a group, for a Coastal Security Conference in Naples, Italy. This signaled the beginning of a dialogue among naval officials in these countries, and produced a joint statement of commitment to support security in the region, improve cooperation, and engage in further discussions at follow-up meetings. Moving this agenda forward will require a stronger consensus within Washington on the threat level, strengthening capacities in the target states, and identifying a viable, regional entity.

Renewed attention in the international community to transparency in oil revenues and expenditures offers a platform to further encourage improved governance and economic reform. The aspirations of African states toward reform and good governance expressed in the NEPAD, Prime Minister Tony Blair's Extractive Industries Transparency Initiative (EITI) and Commission for Africa report, the work of NGOs like Catholic Relief Services on the Chad-Cameroon pipeline, Global Witness in Angola, DATA, the Live-8 concert series, and others, all lay the groundwork for a major international push to incentivize and reward reform efforts. The World Bank and IMF have played a lead role in fostering transparency by upholding standards for staff-monitored programs and conditions for revenue and expenditure disclosures.

The United States and G8 allies will need to reinforce these standards diplomatically to deter countries from shopping for assistance elsewhere in order to avoid conditions of reform. Further, the international community needs to reward reformist elements in countries where reformers confront intractable and sometimes dangerous vested interests and often receive little popular or governmental support. The United States and the international community can bolster that support through debt arrangements, favorable trade financing, and financing for national electrification in exchange for progress in transparency.

Future Engagement with West Africa's Oil Producers

A geopolitical framework is needed to align future U.S. policy toward Africa's energy-rich countries.

COHERENCE

A robust, coherent policy toward the Gulf of Guinea will emphasize high-level, proactive U.S. engagement and a long-term approach that builds U.S. bilateral programmatic support for improved governance across the region, develops a carefully tailored, activist approach to security enhancement, and provides active support to IMF and World Bank transparency and poverty reduction strategies. It will focus on improving communications among U.S. diplomats in the region, Department of Energy officials, and U.S.-based energy companies, on developments that may jeopardize regional stability and the reliability of supply. Various U.S. departments will need to be engaged in this effort, for example: Energy, Interior, Treasury, the Environmental Protection Agency (EPA), and the Coast Guard, among others. It will be no less important to make the Gulf of Guinea policy a regular agenda item in high-level discussions with the EU, the G8, and China.

DIPLOMATIC CAPACITIES

A stronger U.S. diplomatic capacity will permit the intensification of U.S. bilateral engagement with Nigeria, São Tomé and Príncipe,

Gabon, Cameroon, Equatorial Guinea, Chad, and Angola. The United States will need to upgrade U.S. representation in Equatorial Guinea and São Tomé to full embassies and make special efforts to strengthen embassy staffing across the region. Consulates are needed in northern Nigeria and in the Niger Delta, where oil and gas investments are concentrated.

FLEXIBLE RESOURCES

A long-term, well-resourced approach will offer incentives and support for good governance, transparency, and democracy-building, and assist in strengthening capacities to protect fisheries and energy infrastructures, curb criminality, resolve funding issues between central governments and local communities, and manage maritime environments. One component of this approach could be a regional stabilization and governance account, comprising economic support funds, development assistance, foreign military financing, transitional funds, and other accounts flexible enough to respond to the region's diverse challenges. Joint financing of infrastructure or other development projects with oil producing states will promote cooperation and good governance as well as direct oil proceeds to worthwhile objectives.

REGIONAL PARTNERSHIPS

The United States should work to strengthen promising regional initiatives of multilateral agencies like the IMO's cooperative arrangements with regional ports, the Food and Agriculture Organization's efforts to deter illicit fishing in the region, the nascent Gulf of Guinea Commission, and efforts by the AU and the Economic Community of West African States (ECOWAS) in conflict prevention and mediation. The U.S. Coast Guard can expand training of local coast guard counterparts for protection of shipping and offshore structures, and can offer financing to enhance local capacities.

The United States should establish a U.S.-Africa energy forum that would meet regularly and be comprised of interested African governments, energy companies, the World Bank, selected experts, and others. It would provide a forum to discuss evolving market conditions, emerging power generation and other development prospects, maritime and onshore security challenges, and feasible cooperative initiatives.

The New Playing Field:
China's Rising Role

China's Challenge

China's long involvement in Africa predates the independence period of the 1960s, but the current level and intent of China's involvement is different. China has emerged as a significant world player on the economic scene, with an ever-growing demand for oil, timber, minerals, and other natural resources. China comes to Africa in the twenty-first century not only with a need for these natural resources, but also with the financial resources and political influence to pursue its objectives vigorously. Other Asian states with rising economies are following China's lead, including India, Malaysia, and South Korea. China has altered the strategic context in Africa.

All across Africa today, China is acquiring control of natural resource assets, outbidding Western contractors on major infrastructure projects, and providing soft loans and other incentives to bolster its competitive advantage. China's demand for resources is driving up the world price for several commodities, such as copper, gold, aluminum, nickel, and timber, reversing a long decline and giving African exporters of these materials a welcome economic boost. China, however, also contributes to serious environmental damage in Africa, especially in its timber activities. Its burgeoning textile exports are also undermining Africa's recent growth in this sector.

Perhaps most disturbing to U.S. political objectives is China's willingness to use its seat on the UN Security Council to protect some of Africa's most egregious regimes from international sanction, in particular Sudan and Zimbabwe. China offers an alternative source of support, even for some of the United States' closest allies, when they chafe under Western pressure for economic or political reform. Ethiopia, criticized because of recent election irregularities and its continuing border dispute with Eritrea, called China "its most reliable [trading] partner" and indicated interest in closer military cooperation. President Mwai Kibaki of Kenya, under pressure from Western donors because of corruption in his administration, led a high-level delegation to China to seek investment and aid. Angola has largely resisted IMF and other aid donors' recommendations for economic reforms after receiving more than $2 billion in soft loans from China.

China's Evolving Role

In the early period of African independence, China's intentions were primarily diplomatic. China increased diplomatic overtures to Africans to counter recognition of Taiwan as the representative of China and to shore up votes for the eventual rejection of Taiwan's China credentials in the UN. Another Chinese objective was to compete with both Western and Russian influence. In Zimbabwe, China backed the liberation movement of Robert Mugabe, while Russia backed that of Joshua Nkomo. President Mugabe's ultimate election victory laid the foundation for the close relationship that exists between China and Zimbabwe today.

China's image as a developing country—indeed, as a member of the Third World fraternity—was and remains an important part of its appeal. Developing countries include China in the "Group of 77 plus China," actually a group of more than 130 nations that focuses on globalization, South-South cooperation, and North-South relations. China is lauded, in contrast to other donors, for not conditioning its aid on governance, human rights, or economic policy. As Ambassador David Shinn said in testimony before the U.S.-China Commission in July 2005, developing countries consider China the only permanent member of the UN Security Council to be "one of their own." It is an image on which China trades heavily.

In 2000, China created the China-Africa Cooperation Forum (CACF), which meets at the ministerial level every three years. At its second meeting in Addis Ababa in 2003, Chinese Premier Wen Jiabao announced that China had cancelled the debt of thirty-one African countries totaling $1.3 billion, promised support for NEPAD, and increased participation in UN peacekeeping operations in Africa. He supported Africa's position on multilateralism, the elimination of trade barriers and farm subsidies, and increased aid and debt relief by the developed countries. He promised China would gradually increase aid to Africa, provide professional training for 10,000 Africans over three years, including military officers, grant duty-free access to Africa's least-developed countries, increase tourism, and encourage Chinese firms to invest in Africa. These promises are being kept. Thousands of Africans are currently studying in China, and China has expanded its aid and business interests across the continent. As of November 30, 2005, China had contributed 899 peacekeepers to eight UN missions in Africa. Additionally, there are 900 Chinese doctors serving in Africa, and China has begun developing a malaria vaccine program in East Africa.

China's Energy Interests

As David Zweig and Bi Jianhai noted in the September/October 2005 issue of *Foreign Affairs*, "An unprecedented need for resources is now driving China's foreign policy." China, now the world's second largest importer of oil, accounts for 31 percent of global growth in oil demand. China imports 28 percent of its oil from Africa, mostly from Angola, Sudan, and Congo. But China is active in every part of Africa, seeking exploration rights, ownership of facilities, and import agreements.

Sudan

Sudan is a special case because it illustrates how China can benefit from Western concerns over terrorism and human rights. It also illustrates what has been referred to as China's willingness to offer a "total package: cash, technology, and political protection from international pressures."

Since the late 1980s, U.S. concerns over Khartoum's tactics in the war against the south and its ties to terrorist groups persuaded many Western oil companies to withdraw from Sudan. Until 1996, Osama bin Laden lived in Sudan, and several terrorist attacks had been arranged in or launched from Sudan. Although Chevron had invested $1 billion in exploration that confirmed more than one billion barrels of proven reserves, in 1989 the company sold its shares back to the government of Sudan. Canada's Talisman entered the Sudanese oil arena, but, under pressure from the United States and public opinion at home, it sold its interests to an Indian company.

China, Malaysia, and India quickly filled the gap left by Western companies. In 1996, the CNPC took a 40 percent interest as part of a consortium to develop Sudan's Heglig and Unity oil fields. In 1998, the CNPC's construction arm participated in building a 930-mile long pipeline from those oil fields to the Red Sea. It also built a refinery near Khartoum. At one point, China had 10,000 laborers in Sudan to complete CNPC projects. China also controls most of an oil field in southern Darfur, and 41 percent of a field in the Melut Basin. Another Chinese firm is building a pipeline from that field to Port Sudan, where China's Petroleum Engineering Construction Group is constructing a $215 million export tanker terminal. China now gets 7 percent of its oil imports from Sudan.

Economic cooperation extends beyond the oil sector and includes the construction of electric substations and transmission lines; financing for the Kajbar Dam, a $345 million pipeline that will channel water from the Nile to Port Sudan; and a $325 million water system. Chinese investment in Sudan totals about $4 billion, making it Sudan's largest foreign investor. Military cooperation has also grown. Chinese weapons deliveries to Sudan have included ammunition, small arms, towed howitzers, anti-aircraft guns, anti-personnel and anti-tank mines, tanks, helicopters, and fighter aircraft. China also helped establish three weapons factories in Sudan, including one for assembling T-55 tanks. There are also an undetermined number of Chinese military personnel stationed in Sudan to secure its investments.

These activities have taken place while Sudan was under sanctions from the United States and several European countries, and in the midst of civil war and genocide in Darfur. As the Darfur crisis worsened in 2004, China used its position on the UN Security Council to dilute repeated resolutions on the crisis, preventing almost any mention or threat of sanctions against the Sudanese government. Only in March 2005, when world opinion focused on Darfur, did China abstain from voting on a Security Council resolution that referred the possible war crimes and charges of genocide there to the International Criminal Court (ICC) and set in motion a UN study of possible sanctions. The Security Council has not placed sanctions on Sudan.

A new chapter has begun in Sudan, perhaps opening up opportunities for China and the United States to find some common ground. While the Darfur situation remains unresolved, Sudan's north-south civil war has been brought to an end, thanks to high-level diplomatic efforts by the United States in conjunction with European and African governments. Under the peace agreement, the southern Sudan administration will share oil proceeds with the central government and is already exerting direct control over some of the oil concessions in the south. There are also possibilities for new investments, perhaps additional pipelines. At the same time, the south's administrative capacity is weak, and potential problems with small militias, ethnic disputes, and other threats to stability remain. These issues deeply concern the United States.

China also has a stake in seeing the peace agreement succeed and would likely want to improve its relationship with the south, given its strong support of the Khartoum government during the civil war. China has already offered to provide peacekeepers to the UN force scheduled to monitor the agreement. China could contribute further through health programs and badly needed infrastructure projects in the south. A joint Chinese-U.S. investment in new oil facilities is also a possibility.

Relations with Other Oil and Mineral Producers

China has more recently become a significant participant in the oil sector on the west coast of Africa—the largest oil-producing area on the continent. Nigeria and Angola are the main producers and China increased its activities in both countries. In connection with its bid to win exploration rights for a block in Angola, China provided it with a $2 billion soft loan as part of a longer-term aid package. China won the bid.

In July 2005, China and Nigeria signed an $800 million crude oil sale agreement, setting in motion China's purchase of 30,000 barrels a day for five years. Much more significant is that China is expected to win a license to operate four oil blocs in Nigeria, following an agreement to build a hydropower station and take over a privatized Nigerian oil refinery, a money-losing proposition that no Western company was likely to have touched. China is reportedly considering $7 billion in investments in Nigeria, covering a wide variety of sectors including agriculture and also selling fighter jets to Nigeria.

China has taken risks in Nigeria. The oil blocs on which it is bidding on are in contested areas of the Niger Delta region, where insurgency, banditry, and the stealing of oil are endemic. China may lose considerable amounts of money on the refinery, but it will retain a significant foothold in the Nigerian energy sector. China's willingness to invest where the United States and private Western companies are unwilling to go adds to its attraction to African governments.

China is also seeking exploration and development rights in Ethiopia, along the Nigerian-Chad border, and in a number of other countries. In each case, China accompanies its search with investments, infrastructure projects, arms sales, or at least some aid. While favoring Ethiopia, China managed to send arms to both Ethiopia and Eritrea during their 1998 war.

China is Not Alone

The search for natural resources from many quarters is creating a more competitive environment. Other Asian countries with rapidly growing economies are also pursuing access to oil and other natural resources in Africa. India and Malaysia have been active in this area for several years. Now both North Korea and South Korea are getting involved and using similar tactics. South Korea recently won rights to explore an oil bloc in Nigeria by promising to construct a major pipeline and associated facilities, despite Western oil companies' complaints that

Nigeria, in granting the bloc to South Korea, changed the rules for such bidding.

Beyond Oil

Minerals

China is pursuing an active policy in mineral-rich African countries. It is now the world's largest consumer of copper; the United States holds second place. In Zambia, China has invested nearly $170 million in the mining sector, primarily in copper. The Chinese are also active in the DRC, a country gripped by civil war and instability. Despite these conditions, China invests in cobalt and copper mines, began work on roads to facilitate mineral exports, and examined power projects. Similarly, in the midst of a tenuous peace in diamond- and mineral-rich Sierra Leone, China is developing a luxury hotel, investing where others would fear to tread. The Chinese are also considering investment in a titanium mine in Kenya.

The Logging Crisis

Logging and timber are a major focus of Chinese involvement. Here China poses a serious challenge to environmental standards. China is the largest importer of forest products in the world: its imports of forest products have tripled in less than a decade. Many of China's imports from Africa are from unlicensed loggers or from companies with environmentally unsound logging practices condoned by the Chinese. Illegal logging is devastating some of Africa's forests, and depriving the governments of badly needed revenue.

Illegal timber exports to China from Gabon have been estimated to be as high as 70 percent of Gabon's total timber exports. In Equatorial Guinea, the American Forest & Paper Association estimates that up to 90 percent of the total harvest going to China is illegal. Although Mozambique instituted a system of "simple license" forest concessions that restrict Mozambican loggers to a limited amount of timber, this system is being abused. According to testimony by Allan Thornton, president of the Environmental Investigation Agency, a nonprofit environmental organization, Chinese middlemen hire local license holders to cut the timber and then ship it through informal ports along the coast. The timber is then transferred to Chinese ships offshore. In Central Africa, a firm linked to China was fined over $1.3 million for what has been called "anarchic logging," including cutting undersized trees, logging outside legal boundaries, and logging in unallocated concessions.

China was a major importer of Liberian timber during Charles Taylor's rule. Taylor, who has since been indicted by the UN court in Sierra Leone for financing and fostering that country's brutal civil war, relied heavily on timber resources to support his own military efforts and to fund mercenaries in both Sierra Leone and Ivory Coast. By 2001, China was Liberia's largest buyer of wood products. According to a report commissioned by USAID, harvested timber was transported to Liberian ports and bartered to the Chinese and others for weapons and munitions. On May 6, 2003, the UN Security Council imposed an embargo on Liberian timber products. Chinese imports plunged thereafter and appear to have ended in 2004.

Other Businesses

Chinese companies own diversified investments in Africa. Some of these are profit-making, but others seem aimed at establishing positions of influence and staking out future opportunities. Thirty Chinese companies reportedly invested in Kenya during the first half of 2004. Following the donation of communications equipment to Telkom Kenya and the Kenya Broadcasting Corporation, China won contracts to install 26,000 switching lines for Telkom Kenya, improve the telecommunications facilities at Safaricom, and sell cranes for the port of Mombasa. In Ethiopia, Chinese companies bid aggressively on infrastructure projects. The head of one Chinese company admitted to a South African reporter that his orders from Beijing were to bid low, regardless of the impact on profitability.

In Uganda, a Chinese pharmaceutical firm is introducing a new anti-malaria drug and bidding on a contract to supply treated mosquito bed nets. China is planning to test a malaria vaccine in other African countries. China's growing involvement in malaria parallels that of the United States. Some one million people, mostly children, die each year from malaria in Africa. President Bush recently announced a $1.2 billion anti-malaria initiative. Western pharmaceutical companies are also testing malaria vaccines. This could be an area of cooperation rather than competition between the United States and China.

A Mixed Bag

Africa's Gain

Africa has profited from economic growth in Asia and its subsequent growth in demand for oil and other natural resources. African oil producers, in particular, have received a substantial windfall. Nigeria might not have been able to negotiate such a favorable debt relief program from the Paris Club this year, eliminating some $18 billion in debt, if recent oil price increases had not allowed it to offer $6 billion to clear interest and past arrears as required by the deal. Copper exporters like Zambia and the DRC are likewise encouraged since copper prices have reached their highest level in sixteen years.

China is also investing and providing assistance in areas that Western aid agencies and private investors have long neglected: physical infrastructure, industry, and agriculture. USAID has not funded heavy infrastructure projects since the late 1970s. Both USAID and the World Bank reduced assistance to agriculture by as much as 90 percent in the 1990s. Yet these are areas that are once again recognized as essential for Africa's growth. U.S. companies are also most heavily invested in the extractive industries, whereas Chinese companies are eager to go into many other fields. Finally, China offers African nations alternative financing to Western donors, emboldening some leaders to take a harder look at the conditionality of the IMF and other institutions, advice that may or may not be best for their circumstances.

Africa's Loss

China's principal interest in the continent is access to natural resources. But Africa also provides new markets for China's growing economy. Chinese trade with Africa has risen sharply, from $10 billion in 2003 to $20 billion in 2004, and another 50 percent increase is estimated for 2005. Chinese consumer goods are flooding African markets, and—

as in the United States—there has been growing concern about the effect on local industries. Chinese textiles exports to Africa are undermining local industry, while the growth of Chinese exports to the United States is shutting down the promising growth of African exports in this field. The negative impact on African exports comes from the ending of the Multifiber Agreement (MFA), which had allowed the United States to place quotas on clothing and textile imports from China. The United States enacted AGOA in 2000, which gave African countries almost unlimited access to the U.S. market. Textiles were one of the fastest growing exports under AGOA, with rapid growth in countries like Lesotho, Swaziland, Ghana, Uganda, and Kenya. Once the MFA expired in January 2005, however, Chinese exports to the United States soared and African exporters found that they could not compete.

Southern Africa provides a good example of these effects. Chinese textile exports to South Africa grew from 40 percent of clothing imports to 80 percent by the end of 2004. By the end of 2002, 75,000 people had lost their jobs in South Africa's textile industry. More than ten clothing factories in Lesotho closed in 2005, forcing at least 10,000 employees out of work. South Africa's clothing exports to the United States dropped from $26 million in the first quarter of 2004 to $12 million in the first quarter of 2005. South African industrialists and workers have clamored for protective action, joined by church leaders and opposition leader Tony Leon. Affected companies are calling for customs officials to impound undervalued Chinese imports.

In Nigeria, low-cost imports have devastated the textile and other consumer product industries of Kano and Kaduna. In these largely Muslim cities, one Nigerian parliamentarian described the frightening situation of vast numbers of unemployed youth as a powder keg in Nigeria's already fractured society. Given Nigeria's underdeveloped and unreliable power supply, which forces most industries to rely on back-up diesel generators, the prospect of Nigeria regaining a competitive edge seems remote.

Implications for the United States

China's rise in Africa poses three challenges to the United States and its Western partners. The first is China's protection of "rogue states" like

Sudan and Zimbabwe in the face of egregious human rights violations. Second is China's effect on patterns of Western influence: negative pressures—such as withholding aid or placing limitations on investments—to improve an African country's human rights or governing practices provide less leverage if China is prepared to counterbalance that influence. Third, Chinese business practices, which serve state interests as much as a profit motive, create unfair competition to U.S. firms in bidding for contracts. This may become a more contentious issue with expected increases in overall aid to Africa and the number of contracts up for bid.

Protection of Rogue States

As with Sudan, China's interests in Zimbabwe are a mixture of natural resources, historic relationships, and solidarity with developing countries. China is the principal supporter of Robert Mugabe's regime, which is widely criticized in the international community for its ruthless suppression of the opposition and the recent removal of hundreds of thousands of urban residents to rural areas with no regard for life, health, or satisfactory alternative arrangements. China has continued investing in minerals, roads, farming, and supplying Mugabe with jets and other armaments. "Zimbabwe is all but owned by China," says one observer quoted in a South African article. "In return for a rare hand of friendship in an increasingly hostile world, Mugabe has offered Chinese companies almost anything they want, regardless of payback."[1] Nevertheless, China's support of Mugabe is not unlimited. In the wake of a report from the UN denouncing Mugabe's urban removals, China appears to have rebuffed Mugabe's request for substantial aid to meet his overdue obligations to the IMF.

Changing Patterns of Influence

Issues of transparency, corruption, improved government services, and sound economic policies, while less dramatic than gross instances of human rights violations, are critically important in many countries in

---

[1] "PanAfrica: Chinese the New Economic Imperialists in Africa," *Business Day*, February 21, 2005.

Africa. The United States, the other members of the G8, and advocacy groups have been especially active in promoting transparency in the oil and mineral sectors of developing countries. This is the focus of EITI, a tripartite program of governments, industries, and NGOs led by the United Kingdom, and of a similar initiative in the G8 Africa Action Plan. Greater transparency and more equitable use of oil and mineral proceeds are vital to the stability as well as the long-term health of producing countries.

China's aid and investments, however, are attractive to Africans precisely because they come with no conditionality related to governance, fiscal probity, or the other concerns of Western donors. China proudly touts its approach. China's deputy foreign minister, Zhou Wenzhong, told an interviewer, "Business is business. We try to separate politics from business. . . . You [the West] have tried to impose a market economy and multiparty democracy on these countries which are not ready for it. We are also against embargoes, which you have tried to use against us."[2]

Angola is a prominent example. The IMF and Western countries have been pressing Angola to improve the transparency of its oil sector and to make other reforms as prelude to a planned aid donor's conference. However, in the wake of China's $2 billion loan, along with rising oil prices, Angola seems less concerned with a formal agreement with the IMF or interested in substantial aid if conditioned. Angola's ambassador to South Africa remarked that making transparency a condition for the donors' conference was "uncalled for."[3] Angola has indicated that India and Brazil are interested in making loans similar to China's. Angola is prepared to look to even more controversial sources of investment. North Korea recently sent a mission to Angola to look into exploration for uranium.

China thus presents a challenge in an area where U.S. political leverage was once significant—the oil and gas sectors. Members of Congress recently criticized Western oil companies for doing business

---

[2] Howard W. French, "China in Africa: All Trade and No Political Baggage," *New York Times,* August 8, 2004.

[3] "Angola: Donors' Conference Likely to be Delayed Over Oil Accounts," *Southscan (London),* June 30, 2005, viewed July 6, 2005 at http://allafrica.com/stories/printable/2005070671.html.

in Equatorial Guinea, a small country with a poor human rights record. Yet, if U.S. companies withdraw, Equatorial Guinea would quickly have other suitors. The same is true for other countries with new-found oil and gas reserves, such as Mauritania. China may lack some of the technology for deep water production that these countries need, but it is actively seeking partnerships with U.S. and European firms to overcome this disadvantage. In Angola, BP and China's state-owned oil company have already entered into a joint venture.

Business Competition

China utilizes a variety of instruments to advance its interests that are not available to the United States or to U.S. companies. Most of China's investments are through state-owned companies, whose individual investments do not have to be profitable if they serve national Chinese objectives. China's companies may therefore bid low, even at a loss, for major contracts. The United States does not combine offers of aid with private investment ventures; indeed, such practices are discouraged by most major donors under principles enunciated by the Organization for Economic Cooperation and Development (OECD). As aid programs expand in Africa, especially for large infrastructure, telecommunication projects, and industrial development, U.S. companies may begin to complain more loudly about what appears to be unfair competition for contracts, adding to the issues the United States will have to raise with Africa and with China. Again, it is not China alone but others, like South Korea, that will challenge the position in these markets and the traditional competitive advantages the United States and European countries have enjoyed.

Policy Response

It would be easy, but mistaken, to consider China an adversary in Africa. Like other growing economies, China is a legitimate competitor for natural resources. It is necessary to recognize that the rise of China, India, and other Asian countries changes the strategic and economic environment in Africa. The United States and Europe cannot consider Africa their *chasse gardé*, as the French once saw francophone Africa. The rules are changing as China seeks not only to gain access to resources, but also to control resource production and distribution, perhaps positioning itself for priority access as these resources become scarcer. In adapting to the changing circumstances, China has become a savvy competitor.

The United States nevertheless retains many advantages on which to build. There is a large reservoir of good will toward the United States in Africa as well as recognition of the importance of the United States to Africa's hopes for a larger role in the global economy. Despite new investment from Asia, the United States, the United Kingdom, and France still account for 70 percent of foreign direct investment in Africa. U.S. oil companies still lead in the offshore extraction technology critical to West Africa's growing energy production. The United States continues to import substantially from African oil and gas producers, and the market is still controlled more by international supply and demand than by any individual country's manipulations.

These are assets on which to build positively. Thus, the answer is not for the United States to ignore issues of governance, transparency, or human rights, but to compete for the support and partnership of African leaders, in oil producing states and elsewhere on the continent, who also care about these issues and need U.S. support and encouragement to promote them. Such partners exist, but threats of divestment or cutting off of aid are not likely to be effective instruments for motivating them.

Aid programs should not be distorted into vehicles for supporting U.S. companies abroad. The OECD principles in this regard are sound. But the United States has instruments, such as the Export-Import Bank, OPIC, and the United States Trade and Development Agency (USTDA), which can be used more in a proactive and coordinated manner to assist U.S. companies to compete in this changing environment. Furthermore, U.S. aid programs should consider returning to investment in infrastructure projects, which are now identified to be of major importance to economic growth in Africa. In that sector, the potential for public-private partnerships, consistent with sound development principles, may well be possible.

Finally, China is not impervious to world opinion or to its image as a world power. It has pulled back from unqualified support for Sudan and Zimbabwe in the face of world opinion and bowed to UN sanctions against Liberia. It rarely uses its veto in the UN, and then mostly when the issue relates to Taiwan. It has become a significant contributor to UN peacekeeping. The door may well be open to a frank dialogue on the situation in Africa, including those differences and common interests that concern the United States.

There are many ways in which the United States can compete more vigorously and effectively with China and other new players in Africa, both to preserve its influence and thwart deterrents to progress on economic and political reform. There is an urgent need to do so; to bet on China's influence simply waning over time would be a mistake.

Security and Terrorism Concerns

Trends Toward Radical Islamic Terrorism: How Real Is the Threat?

Africa, especially the Horn of Africa, has a long history of externally inspired terror that threatens both domestic and Western interests. In 1973, pro-Palestinian militants murdered the U.S. ambassador and deputy chief of the mission in Khartoum, and in 1980 they bombed the Norfolk Hotel in Nairobi, Kenya, killing fifteen. The former was in retaliation for the September 1970 expulsions of Palestinians from Jordan, the latter for Kenyan cooperation in the 1976 Israeli Entebbe raid. In both instances, and others like it during this period, terror was understood as an alien import, transitory in nature.

Over the past fifteen years, terror in East Africa has increasingly been fed by a radical Islamist agenda. Terrorist organizations operating from the Middle East and South Asia are seeking to utilize their funds, leadership, and training to develop terrorist cells and links to emergent indigenous networks within Africa's 300 million-strong Muslim population. One recent analysis of foreign jihadists in Iraq estimates that 25 percent originated in Africa, principally North Africa, though an increasing share comes from sub-Saharan Africa. The U.S. Central Command (CENTCOM) recently announced that it anticipates a high back-migration into the Horn of trained jihadists. This Islamist threat vies for attention in many African settings with more immediate, domestically driven sources of conflict, including the Lord's Resistance Army

(LRA) of northern Uganda and the Democratic Forces for the Liberation of Rwanda (FDLR).

An active debate is ongoing today in Africa over how much of a true threat radical Islam poses and to what degree it has established enduring domestic roots. That debate often becomes entangled in and, at times, distorted by widespread skepticism regarding U.S. intentions.

Between 1991 and 1996, Osama bin Laden made Sudan the center of his expansive global ambitions, in league with the Sudanese charismatic extremist leader, Hassan al-Turabi. After bin Laden's expulsion to Afghanistan in 1996, a regional network lived on, with ties to the Al-Ittihad al-Islami movement in Somalia and to the small core led by Mohammed al-Fasul in Kenya, along with linkages to South Asia and the East African archipelago (Comoros, Zanzibar, and Lamu). That diverse assembly of interests engineered the U.S. embassy bombings in Nairobi and Dar es Salaam, Tanzania, which left 224 dead and thousands gravely injured in August 1998. The same network was responsible for the attacks in Mombasa, Kenya, in November 2002 that killed sixteen and came perilously close to taking down an Israeli airliner with more than 200 passengers.

In retrospect, the model of loosely affiliated groups that opportunistically combine indigenous and external actors, has been refined in the Horn during the past decade. Today, it is a predominant model among Islamist extremists who have struck in Britain, Spain, Morocco, Egypt, and elsewhere, and who pose a continuing threat.

Outside the Horn, an Algerian movement, the Salafist Group for Preaching and Combat (GSPC), has attempted to enlist and train adherents from among neighboring Sahelian states, making use of trans-Sahara smuggling routes, the region's vast ungoverned spaces, and the ample ransom it acquired in 2003 for eighteen European hostages. Whether the GSPC poses a serious durable threat is a subject of ongoing debate. Most recently, in June 2005 the GSPC ambushed and killed fourteen Mauritanian soldiers. The United States has officially designated the GSPC as a terrorist organization and instituted sanctions against it.

Exploiting Muslim Ties

In both Nigeria and South Africa in recent years, there have been credible reports that diverse outside radical Islamists continue to test opportunities to form local partnerships to strike at both official and private Western targets. They have sought to take advantage of complex, sizeable Muslim populations (half of Nigeria's 130 million citizens, two million of South Africa's forty-five million citizens) with linkages to the Middle East and South Asia, local radical traditions (e.g., People Against Gangsterism and Drugs [PAGAD] in South Africa), disaffection with domestic policies perceived as discriminatory or offensively aligned with the West, and hostility toward the United States.

Northern Nigeria, where there is no official U.S. diplomatic or commercial presence, is of special concern. Twelve of its thirty-six states operate under Sharia law, northern former military officers see themselves as disenfranchised since the return to democratic rule in 1999, and a youth bulge confronts worsening unemployment and disaffection. There is easy access into northern Nigeria from Yemen, Saudi Arabia, and Sudan through Chad.

South Africa's and Nigeria's comparatively superior air transport, communications, and banking infrastructures are a powerful allure, as is the ability to enter at will and buy one's way forward. While some individuals and cells have been apprehended or disrupted, few informed experts are confident that authorities of either country have the threat within their midst under control.

On the continent, U.S. vulnerability to terror is aggravated by special circumstances. Most U.S. embassies, commercial facilities (especially the expansive energy sector), and humanitarian organizations in Africa are less protected than in other areas of the world and are conspicuous soft targets. Host governments typically lack the essential capacities to monitor, interdict, and prosecute suspected terrorists. Weak or failing anarchic states provide havens, recruiting grounds, and transit opportunities for terrorist groups and Africa's burgeoning criminal organizations. In strong states like Nigeria and South Africa, as well as many West African coastal states, elaborate crime syndicates have become ever more adept in laundering money and trafficking humans, arms, drugs, oil, timber, and diamonds.

The U.S. Approach, Mostly a Military Matter

In the aftermath of the 1998 embassy bombings, the United States broadened counterterror cooperation with Kenya, Tanzania, Ethiopia,

and Uganda and, in the spring of 2000, it opened a dialogue with
Sudan. In retrospect, America's quiet investment in these relations
created a valuable base for future expanded cooperation. In many
other parts of Africa, however, U.S. intelligence capacities decayed
precipitously during the 1990s, following the end of the Cold War.
Critical uncovered gaps arose in northern Nigeria and Somalia.

Post-9/11, the U.S. counterterror approach to Africa has been led
by the U.S. military: CENTCOM in the Horn; EUCOM in West,
Central, and southern Africa; and the U.S. Special Operations Command (SOCOM). More quietly, U.S. intelligence cooperation with
key states has expanded in parallel with the enlargement of the U.S.
military's role. The increased U.S. attention to African security through
these initiatives has resulted in several highly valuable programs that
warrant continued support to ensure they remain robust and effective.
More effort is also required to achieve stronger diplomatic supervision
of U.S. counterterror efforts, along with public diplomacy to establish
trust within Muslim communities. Counterterror initiatives are frequently undertaken with inadequate consideration of whether these
operations will build durable partnerships and create true capacities
within partner governments, as well as how they might have an impact
on civil liberties, democratic governance, and popular perceptions of
U.S. intentions. Also, initiatives fail to consider how to mitigate the
risk that host governments will be tempted to use the relationship that
develops from an emerging security alliance with the United States as
an excuse for egregious misrule.

Recent events in Mauritania provided a powerfully sobering example of the hazards for U.S. policy. The recently deposed President Ely
Ould Mohamed Taya exploited his allegiance with the United States
and Israel as he imprisoned rivals, branded the opposition as Islamic
extremists, and rigged elections. When overthrown in a coup in July
2005, popular opinion swung behind the new strongman, Ould Vall.
For U.S. policymakers, as well as AU members, this sudden outcome
stirred a scramble to rebalance counterterror and democratic concerns.
A similar risk is involved in EUCOM's cooperation with Chad, whose
president is seeking a constitutional amendment that would enable
him to become president for life, where considerable internal unrest
is possible.

In Djibouti, the Combined Joint Task Force-Horn of Africa, staffed with 1,200 to 1,800 soldiers, provides a long-term interdiction and strike force, with some limited training capacity, and outreach programs to the local communities in the region. By and large it is a creative, good-faith proactive effort to shape the environment in a preventive manner. Its active mission, however, beyond a reserve capacity, remains somewhat ambiguous. A complementary $100 million U.S.-East Africa counterterror initiative, introduced in mid-2003, aims to build both civilian and security capacities, principally within Kenya and Ethiopia. These bilateral collaborations have advanced significantly, though they have been prone to periodic setbacks, as seen in Kenya, where corruption and a weak judiciary recently undermined prosecution in 2004 of those responsible for the Mombasa attacks. In Ethiopia they may be affected by the recent political unrest.

In Sudan, a U.S. team has secured substantial cooperation from the Sudanese government in pursuit of al-Qaeda and affiliated suspects, aided considerably, from late 2001 to mid-2003, by the threat of U.S. military action against Khartoum. In general, this track was kept separate from U.S. involvement in the peace process to end the north-south civil war and later from its international engagement on Darfur. In April 2005, however, that broke down temporarily when the Central Intelligence Agency (CIA) flew the senior Sudanese intelligence chief, Major General Salah Abdallah Gosh, who was thought to be seriously implicated in the Janjaweed militia campaign of violence against civilians in Darfur, to Washington for high-level consultations. Not surprisingly, this resulted in uproar on Capitol Hill and in the Department of State.

In West Africa, EUCOM has established several forward-operating locations (in Senegal, Gabon, Mali, Ghana, Uganda, Namibia, and South Africa) involving the upgrade of ports and airfields, prepositioning of fuel and other critical supplies, and access agreements that permit swift deployment of U.S. forces for counterterror purposes. In 2005, the United States launched the TSCTI, an ambitious five-year $500 million program, which is not yet fully funded and is intended to build North and sub-Saharan Africa capacities to patrol borders, interdict armed groups, and cooperate intraregionally (in Algeria, Chad, Mali, Morocco, Tunisia, Nigeria, Senegal, Ghana, Niger, and Mauritania).

Unlike the precursor PSI, TSCI is planned as a holistic, multifaceted program in which no more than 20 to 30 percent of the funds would be for military cooperation. Public diplomacy, economic activities, law enforcement, and intelligence cooperation are all to be included. How such programs are to be coordinated with other embassy and USAID programs in the region, and separated from military activities, remains unclear. In June 2005, a kick-off regional exercise, *Operation Flintlock*, involved over 1,000 U.S. Special Forces. EUCOM has also, over the past two years, developed the outlines of a multilateral initiative to strengthen maritime security in the energy-rich Gulf of Guinea. That plan awaits refinement and approval at higher levels in Washington.

Ensuring an Effective Counterterrorism Strategy in the Future

A successful U.S. counterterror strategy for Africa requires a forward-looking, long-term investment, concentrated on rebuilding depleted U.S. intelligence capacities and forming stable partnerships with key host governments that will create enduring African capacities to detect, deter, and interdict threats, and prosecute those responsible. These goals each require patience and realism. They will only be realized through incremental, concerted efforts over several years.

Improving Policy Coordination

Problems of balance and ambiguity in the counterterrorism programs to date arise from a dysfunctional interagency process in Washington as much, if not more, from problems in the field. Counterterrorism policy in Africa needs to be developed and directed by an interagency process that balances the military, diplomatic, economic, and informational aspects of the policy, and provides guidance to the various missions and commands in the field.

Strengthening Capacities

U.S. intelligence assets worldwide are severely stretched, by developments in the Middle East, South Asia, and Europe. In Africa, priority should be given to eliminating the critical U.S. gaps in northern Nigeria and Somalia. Diplomats trained in relevant languages are sorely needed to work in northern Nigeria and the Sahel in order to maintain contact and to understand developments there. The Task Force endorses the recommendation, made earlier in 2005 by the Council Task Force on post-conflict capabilities, that there should be a special cell created within the intelligence community to improve collection and analysis on weak and failed states.[4]

The United States has learned that while there has been progress in building trust and cooperation with South Africa and Nigeria in recent years, it has been a delicate process, and special care needs to be taken to consolidate these key ties. As seen in the Kenyan trials following the Mombasa attack, the effort to build internal capacities among existing partners is vulnerable to corruption and sudden setbacks; a long-term strategy will need to anticipate and prepare for this risk.

The Correct Diplomatic Strategy

A broader, more balanced, and diplomatically driven approach will also be essential to success.

It will be important to lower the profile of U.S. uniformed personnel, while placing in the lead senior officials charged with articulating an integrated counterterrorism vision that speaks more directly to the importance of redressing locally perceived threats such as criminal networks and weapons trafficking; demonstrates greater sensitivity to human rights, democratic governance, and public opinion; and ensures there is a much higher investment in public diplomacy that reaches Muslim populations and counteracts the widespread skepticism of U.S. actions. Police, intelligence, and investigative training of the type that has been undertaken already in East Africa should also complement continued military assistance.

---

[4]See *In the Wake of War: Improving U.S. Post-Conflict Capabilities, Report of an Independent Task Force* (New York: Council on Foreign Relations Press, 2005), p. 24.

The HIV/AIDS Pandemic

The Pandemic's Toll in Africa

The profound toll of HIV/AIDS upon Africa is rapidly gathering force as this maturing pandemic enters an advanced stage. The huge spike of new HIV infections in the early 1990s is today translating, a decade later, into millions of persons now symptomatic with AIDS. They are concentrated in high-prevalence states in eastern and southern Africa. Death rates are now accelerating, with potentially deeply destabilizing effects. At the same time, popular pressures are intensifying for access to life-extending treatment.

In the most gravely impacted countries, the pandemic has reversed a generation of gains in human development, hitting young and middle-aged adults of all socioeconomic classes and leaving a dangerous youth bulge. The annual cost in foregone economic growth is estimated from 1 percent to 2 percent. Life expectancy has dropped precipitously by as much as twenty-five years. Losses among key professional groups, such as educators and health care providers, are exceptionally high. And young women and girls, who account today for 60 percent of new HIV infections, are acutely vulnerable due to fundamental inequities, including lack of control over their sexual activity. As the pandemic has damaged national economies, undermined communities, and destroyed the livelihoods of households, it has worsened poverty and raised the specter that in the near future the provision of basic services by some national governments may become unfeasible.[5]

[5]See Laurie Garrett, *HIV and National Security: Where are the Links?* (New York: Council on Foreign Relations Press, 2005).

Twenty-six million of the more than forty million persons living with HIV are Africans. More than twenty-five million persons are estimated to have died of HIV/AIDS worldwide, the vast majority in Africa. While treatment and care are expanding rapidly, no more than 10 percent of the population living with HIV actually knows their HIV status. Of the roughly five million persons in Africa who today would hypothetically benefit from life-extending antiretroviral treatment (ART), fewer than 15 percent currently have such access. On the horizon, there are no strong, credible signs that the pandemic's accelerated march is slowing. Each year, almost two million Africans die from AIDS, while over three million more become newly infected.

HIV/AIDS is but one of Africa's acute health challenges. However, since it is so costly and comparatively complex to address, how it is managed now and in the future—the resource flows available, strategies pursued, and institutions constructed—will have a profound bearing on what is possible across a wide range of health needs. In recent years, dramatically expanded efforts on HIV/AIDS by African governments, aided by international donors, have raised hope. In several key countries, these efforts resulted in the promising early launch of treatment, prevention, and care services on a national scale. If managed skillfully, these expanding HIV/AIDS services can contribute to building and strengthening infrastructure that has broad health benefits and that helps consolidate hope and stability in communities. Such gains will make it possible to engage more extensively on public health as a priority in U.S. foreign policy and keep a spotlight on the critical importance of health to Africa's future.

The International Response

In 2005, aggregate spending to control HIV/AIDS is estimated at $8.3 billion, of which two-thirds or more is dedicated to Africa. The United States contributes one-third of these funds. That is a major gain in recent years from the roughly $1 billion aggregate level in 2000 and is attributable to increased mobilization by African governments, now committing over $1 billion annually, and a succession of major international initiatives: most notably, the June 2001 UN General Assembly

Special Session on HIV/AIDS; the 2002 launch of the Global Fund, an independent, international financing mechanism; expanded activities by the World Bank, UNAIDS, and UN operational agencies; PEPFAR; and the rising commitments made by the UK Department for International Development (DFID) and other major donors.

Despite these recent gains, the $8.3 billion now available still falls short of estimated demand. UNAIDS projects that $15 billion will be needed in 2006 to control HIV/AIDS in developing countries, and that this level will rise to $22 billion in 2008. Most of these resources will have to come from international donors. How the United States will sustain a one-third or higher share of commitments is uncertain in the face of these steeply rising demands. Rising U.S. budget deficits, compounded by tax cuts, the war on Iraq, and the aftermath of hurricanes in the southern United States, will create enormous downward pressures on funding for both bilateral and multilateral programs.

The President's Emergency Plan for AIDS Relief

PEPFAR, a $15 billion five-year program, was a response to a broad, bipartisan, consensus within the United States that the global HIV/AIDS pandemic warranted high-level U.S. engagement. It consciously builds upon the foundation of bipartisan support in Congress, mobilized late in the Clinton administration, which expedited the $100 million Leadership and Investment in Fighting an Epidemic (LIFE) initiative in 2000. By late 2005, the bipartisan compact that made the Clinton initiative and, subsequently, the much larger PEPFAR possible has come under increasing strain and is at risk of breakdown. Clashes in the United States, born of ideological and religious differences, intensified with the unfolding implementation of HIV/AIDS treatment, prevention, and care programs. Focused leadership is needed to refortify a pragmatic center committed to consolidating achievements and meeting major emerging challenges.

PEPFAR is a laudable but risky foreign aid initiative. Of the $15 billion for the program, $9 billion are additional new funds. It focuses on twelve African countries, along with Guyana, Haiti, and Vietnam, and sets forth an agenda to bring ART to two million persons; prevent HIV infection among seven million persons; and bring care to ten million persons, including orphans. U.S. HIV/AIDS programs are not limited only to the fifteen focus countries; assistance in some form extends to almost all affected African countries.

The lion's share of resources (55 percent) will go to the provision of ART. In effect, President Bush declared that a signature U.S. foreign policy priority would be the placement of two million individuals vulnerable to AIDS—a disease for which there is no cure or vaccine, and neither in sight—on life-extending care, for an indefinite period. In 2005, the G8 went further, making a commitment on HIV/AIDS to reach "as close as possible to universal access to treatment for all those who need it by 2010."[6]

This was a change in policy. Over the previous fifteen years, the U.S. approach had been almost entirely prevention-oriented. Critical to this change was the radical reduction in per capita annual costs for the provision of ART, from $10,000 at the beginning of the decade to below $1,000, and the emergence of well-organized international campaigns dedicated to expanding access to treatment in developing countries.

Several factors account for the decision by the administration to launch PEPFAR and support the even greater G8 commitment.

Early in this decade, evidence mounted of the scale and gravity of Africa's pandemic. Much-improved data compiled by UNAIDS, the U.S. Bureau of the Census, the U.S. National Intelligence Council, and others confirmed that a huge spike of HIV infections in the 1990s was quickly evolving into a global AIDS pandemic in this decade. The rethinking of the U.S. approach to global security, post-9/11, spelled out in the 2002 National Security Strategy, placed heavy emphasis on global health and the imperative to check the destructive power of runaway global infectious diseases, especially HIV/AIDS. Within Africa, the heightened mobilization of political leadership and internal resources to control HIV/AIDS has demonstrated there are able, committed partners. High media coverage of HIV/AIDS raised public awareness of and deepened interest in the expanding pandemic.

---

[6] "Chair's Summary, Gleneagles Summit," July 8, 2005, at http://www.g8.gc.ca/chairsummary-en.asp.

Changes in U.S. politics also played an integral role. Most pivotal was the shift by religious conservatives in the United States in favor of an activist international engagement to combat HIV/AIDS. Leaders within that community drew attention to the special threat that HIV/AIDS posed to mothers, infants, and orphaned children. They became new de facto partners with the public health and development constituencies already on record in support of expanded HIV/AIDS programs. PEPFAR was able to build further on the bipartisan foundation of support in Congress, mobilized late in the Clinton administration, and expanded through the perseverance of the Congressional Black Caucus. This bipartisan congressional consensus was reinforced by opinion surveys that demonstrated that among Americans there was rising popular knowledge of the pandemic, considerable compassion, and an openness to support enlarged U.S. leadership.

IMPACT ON AFRICA

PEPFAR concentrates on twelve African countries (Botwsana, Mozambique, Namibia, South Africa, Zambia, Ethiopia, Kenya, Rwanda, Tanzania, Uganda, Ivory Coast, and Nigeria) where the pandemic threatens the largest number of people. The United States and other donor HIV/AIDS programs, however, reach nearly every African country. Only a few countries have successfully contained the spread of HIV infections—Uganda and Senegal being the primary examples. For the rest, and particularly in the focal PEPFAR countries, the prospects of rising levels of infection, full blown AIDS, deaths, and potential social and political destabilization continue. In 2004, 2.3 million people in sub-Saharan Africa died from this disease.

Over the course of the first year of operations, differentiated outcomes among the fifteen focal countries began to become apparent, revealing a powerful lesson: At the end of the day, on-the-ground realities in the focal countries selected are decisive to PEPFAR's future outcomes, notwithstanding U.S. policies, funding levels, and programs. It became clear that some serious adjustments to initial PEPFAR program targets would be needed to take account of these realities.

Among small or mid-sized, stable African states with reasonably good leadership, established national polices, working relations with donor governments and implementing organizations, and established operational programs, it has been comparatively straightforward to plan and begin implementation of enlarged treatment, care, and prevention programs. Within this promising pool are Uganda, Kenya, Tanzania, Botswana, Mozambique, Zambia, and Namibia. In most of these countries, the administration has had U.S. ambassadors and agency directors with considerable field knowledge and experience in HIV/AIDS, and a strong passion to do more.

South Africa has posed a paradoxical challenge. Despite exceptional capacities in government, industry, the private health sector, and the nongovernmental sector, it continues to be led by a recalcitrant national government that does not embrace the urgent priority of advancing HIV/AIDS programs. The U.S. embassy there, prescient and well-led, and staffed with an unusual depth of public health expertise, foresaw these challenges early and developed arguably the most comprehensive and sophisticated strategy to circumvent South Africa's special obstacles. A robust civil society and an independent judiciary in South Africa also acted to overcome the government's resistance to providing a broad-scale treatment program. South Africa now spends more than any other African country on HIV/AIDS.

Ethiopia and Nigeria present their own exceptional challenges: large populations (70 million and 130 million respectively), nonexistent or greatly decayed public health systems, delayed action in launching national policies on HIV/AIDS, minimal strength within the nongovernmental sector, and inherent instability born of pervasive corruption in Nigeria and vulnerability to mass famine in Ethiopia. In these two instances, progress in achieving early and midterm goals in treatment, care, and prevention is not out of the question, but is not likely to be near the scale or pace envisioned in the initial targets set by PEPFAR.

EARLY LESSONS LEARNED

In the short span of its existence, PEPFAR has revealed four looming realities:

- White House leadership is essential to achieving quick, major results. Substantial, quick progress in the launch phase (early 2004 to the present) has relied overwhelmingly on concentrated White House leadership, backed by the promise of major new resources and an urgent, strategic purpose, in order to mobilize Congress, multiple agencies, scattered embassies, NGOs, and recipient governments. Absent this factor, the quest to bring programs to a national scale in Africa, and to force diverse agencies within the U.S. government to operate expeditiously and on an altogether different basis of coordination, would never have taken off.

The first year of PEPFAR operations showed results. Country operational plans were developed on a crash basis. Embassy teams were empowered to lead in the refinement of strategies. By early 2005, the administration claimed that it had moved hundreds of millions of dollars in resources, contributed to placing over 230,000 persons on ART, and accelerated the delivery of treatment and prevention programs. Some of these achievements, at least in part, were the result of other investments by African governments and U.S. corporations and foundations' support of treatment programs.

- Mixed reception. PEPFAR has drawn praise from diverse quarters for its determined approach and early results. It has also drawn the following persistent criticisms: (1) the program was introduced without adequate prior consultations with recipient governments, American public health experts, and international organizations already actively engaged in providing HIV/AIDS services; (2) it follows an overwhelmingly bilateral approach that undervalues the integration of U.S. efforts with others and dangerously downgrades U.S. interest in the new multilateral financing instrument, the Global Fund; (3) it focused narrowly on the provision of medical treatment, and too little on the need to build a sustainable public health infrastructure that brings broad benefits and the means to overcome mounting deficits in skilled health workers; and (4) it is hostile to the use of condoms and harms reduction strategies for drug-injecting populations, and does not take a comprehensive enough view of prevention. Alternatively, among political conservatives, especially the religious conservative community, a counterview is that the ABC prevention approach places excessive confidence in the mass distribution of condoms.

• Challenges to achieving mass treatment. There are considerable unknowns related to the true cost of universal procurement, as well as the difficulties of providing treatment on a mass scale. There are also nagging questions such as to how to overcome Africa's growing deficit of skilled health workers and how to mitigate the skewing of health services that will result when a sudden, massive investment is made in HIV/AIDS services.

There is deep uncertainty as to whether it will be possible to ensure a reliable, unbroken logistics chain of affordable ART medications to two million individuals residing in fifteen countries. These countries often have weak institutional environments that are vulnerable to corruption. Also, no one can reliably predict the true, long-term costs of sustainment. It will be essential to account increasingly for individuals who start therapy on less expensive drug regimens and then later require far more expensive, second-line therapy after they have developed side effects or resistance to first-line drugs.

There is also continued confusion over how U.S. procurement of medications for treatment, both patented and generic, will be coordinated with those of the Global Fund, the World Bank, DFID, and others. With no clear plan yet in place for how the administration will deliver low-cost generic medications reliably, safely, and in adequate volumes, U.S. embassies are hard-pressed to explain—to themselves and host governments—how they intend to meet their ambitious targets for expanded treatment.

There is the daunting macro-issue of what will be the true cost for expanded treatment to meet dramatically enlarged demand in the developing world and how these costs will be met. It is wholly plausible that the future costs of delivering and sustaining treatment to an ever-larger population in developing countries will be several times current levels. A premise of UNAIDS estimates for future requirements is that ART will account for an increasing share of total expenditures, assuming new HIV infections continue at the current high rates and that significantly higher numbers of people living with HIV will demand and gain access to treatment. This will extend their lives and add steadily to a population on treatment in the developing world for an indefinite period. This scenario suggests that we may very well be on the edge of explosive demand for ART in the developing world and a sharp ratcheting upwards of long-term carrying costs. These shifts, if they result in widening funding gaps, could stir sharpened tensions between poor countries acutely impacted by HIV/AIDS and the United States and other wealthy Western donors. For the United States, they argue strongly in favor of engaging Congress early on the likely escalating costs for mass treatment and what might be a "fair share" for the United States. They argue also for aggressive early outreach to other donors and countries affected by HIV/AIDS to seek a concerted approach to future escalating demands.

Skilled workforce shortages are also a profound block on the delivery of HIV/AIDS services on a national scale in Africa. Africa will need to more than double its skilled health workers (doctors, nurses, laboratory technicians, and managers) if it is to reach that goal. Greatly expanded training is essential, but the challenge reaches far beyond that. It requires putting in place retention policies that both push back against international commercial recruitment from Africa of skilled personnel and redress poor pay, unsafe working conditions, and weak management. It requires a strategy to minimize the distortion of health services. A sudden surge of funding for HIV/AIDS services can deplete other critical areas, such as child vaccinations and diarrheal disease programs, worsening mortality risks in these areas. Donors, the United States included, have up to now been ill-equipped to face this stark impediment, either through bilateral programs or in concert through multilateral initiatives.

• The obstacles to effective prevention. Prevention must be a priority if the spread of the pandemic is truly to be reversed. The only way that mass treatment can be sustained, moreover, is if the number of new infections is curbed through effective prevention. But ensuring that prevention is a genuine priority and that prevention services are really effective are both formidable challenges. Making the case for providing treatment to extend the lives of persons living with HIV is inherently more immediate and compelling than making the case for preventing HIV infections. One case delivers a tangible service that restores hope for individuals while the other is a non-event.

Further, while much is known about what works to reduce the spread of HIV, there is lack of a strong consensus on how to apply strategies that do work. Indeed, much of the HIV-prevention arena is highly contested societal terrain that inherently invites escalating conflicts around moral and cultural values. At its base, any consideration of HIV/AIDS prevention requires an often-uncomfortable confrontation with intimate aspects of human sexuality—changing behavior of adults and adolescents—and in some countries, with the interaction of sex, illicit drug use, and alcohol. It means inexorably grappling with gender violence and inequality, and the behavior of stigmatized high-risk groups such as commercial sex workers, men who have sex with men, and injection drug users.

The approach to prevention has been made still more complicated by the intensifying suspicion and criticism of PEPFAR, emanating from a diverse range of ideologies and perspectives, and frequently grounded in anecdotes or otherwise thin data. It has centered largely on the clash between advocates of condoms versus advocates of "abstinence only" as a preferred prevention intervention. A related controversy arose in early 2005 when the then Health and Human Services Secretary Tommy Thompson announced that NGO grantees would have to sign a statement condemning commercial sex work, which in turn triggered a lawsuit by DKT International after it lost U.S. funding for prevention programs in Vietnam for refusing to comply with this requirement.

The burgeoning conflict between the different perspectives over prevention came into full view in late August 2005 when AIDS activists alleged that Uganda was experiencing a dire shortage of condoms "that is being driven and exacerbated by PEPFAR and by the extreme policies that the administration in the United States is now pursuing."[7] This incited immediate public counterattacks by U.S. conservatives on U.S. funding for the distribution of condoms.[8]

[7] Comments from the UN secretary-general's special envoy for HIV/AIDS in Africa, Ambassador Stephen Lewis, build on allegations laid out by Jodi Jacobson of the Center for Health and Gender Equity. See Lawrence K. Altman, "U.S. blamed for condom shortage in fighting AIDS in Uganda," *New York Times*, August 30, 2005.

[8] James Dobson, head of Focus on the Family, condemned the U.S.-based group, Advocates for Youth, for promoting condom use in Uganda and reasserted that the dramatic drop in its HIV prevalence was due to abstinence. In an earlier development, Senator Tom Coburn (R-

These episodes have created a loud background noise that has hard-ened opinion and conjured false choices, edged out consideration of many important prevention issues such as gender, alcohol abuse, and injection drug use, and obscured the debate over PEPFAR's long-term requirements.

This escalating confrontation could move in two directions. The two new de facto partners in support of expanded HIV/AIDS programs—secular and religious—could find sufficient common purpose, manage their differences, and strengthen the bipartisan compact that made PEPFAR possible. To its credit, PEPFAR has been reaching out to critics on both sides to present a balanced and increasingly comprehensive approach. Alternatively, the two constituencies could grow more antagonistic as implementation pro-ceeds, battling over implementation on the airwaves and in Congress. Ultimately, under the latter scenario, the political center will fray as will prospects for future sustained, high-level U.S. leadership on HIV/AIDS.

Risks to the Nascent International Harmonization Effort

The Global Fund was launched in 2002 with heavy U.S. political and financial backing. It seeks to cover a financing gap—estimated at between $7 billion and $9 billion in 2002—for these diseases. By summer 2005, the Global Fund had committed $3.7 billion to over 300 programs in 127 countries. Sixty percent of its funds went to Africa and 55 percent to fight HIV/AIDS. As of September 2005, the Global Fund had moved $1.5 billion to field projects, contributing to 220,000 persons receiving ART, 600,000 people receiving treatment for tuber-culosis, and 1.1 million people being treated for malaria.

With the launch of PEPFAR in 2003, the Global Fund's relationship to the United States became more complicated and at times difficult. The administration has publicly acknowledged the Global Fund's special strengths and capacities and its value as a partner. It can leverage resources

OK) demanded that the United States cease financing a prevention program by Population Services International in Central America that promoted condom use. See William Fisher, "Politics: U.S. Conservatives Step Up Fight Against Condom Programs," *Inter Press Service*, September 1, 2005.

from multiple sources, finance tuberculosis and malaria programs in PEPFAR focus countries, and support a range of infectious disease programs in countries that are important to the United States, but fall outside of PEPFAR.

Tensions are inherent in the relationship, however, since the Global Fund and PEPFAR are in competition for scarce dollars. That competition appears increasingly zero-sum, especially as PEPFAR programs rapidly expand and require ever more funding at the same time that pressures intensify upon the Global Fund to graduate to the scale of operations originally envisioned by its founders. This inherent competition prompted skeptics within the administration to emphasize the Global Fund's slow disbursement rates and criticize its other flaws. It lacks operational or technical capacities and is wholly reliant on in-country partners. It also lacks a track record for control over corruption, initially had weak fundraising successes with European donors and Japan, and is vulnerable to multiple political pressures. To the Global Fund's credit, its management sought to answer each of these concerns promptly, as best it could during the Global Fund's start-up phase, and quickly put in place impressive, transparent reporting mechanisms on its website, superior to virtually all bilateral donors, including the United States.

In the initial allocation plan for PEPFAR's $15 billion, annual contributions to the Global Fund from PEPFAR were set at $200 million, far less than the $300 million committed in the start-up year between 2001 and 2002, or the $322 million committed in 2003. Beginning in 2003, finding a proper balance between the U.S. bilateral program and the Global Fund fell to congressional appropriators, who were generous and protective of the Global Fund (allocating $458 million in 2004 and $435 million in 2005).

Beginning in FY 2004, Congress also officially mandated that the U.S. contribution could not exceed one-third of the total funds raised. That prompted the Global Fund's leadership to become more aggressive in fundraising, scoring major gains from the Japanese, Canadians, French, and Germans in the lead-up to the 2005 G8 Summit at Gleneagles. Achieving these results has proven increasingly problematic. At the September 2005 meeting to replenish funding for the Global Fund's existing projects, donors pledged only $3.7 billion toward the estimated requirement of $7.1 billion. While European, most notably French, and Japanese donations were up significantly, the U.S. annual contribution, at $300 million for each of the next two years, amounted to far less than one-third of funds pledged. It now remains to be seen whether Congress will raise that number significantly. The disappointing replenishment outcome not only called into question the "fair shares" compact, but also the ability of the Global Fund to sustain its existing project commitments and, beyond that, to fund new projects to meet emerging demands in the next two years. For the latter, there are no pledged funds and the next funding round has been set for mid-2006.

On the broader international front, the administration had mixed experiences at the onset of PEPFAR that revealed the high value of investing in health diplomacy. The Bangkok Global AIDS conference of July 2004 was a diplomatic and public relations nadir. Little credit was given to U.S. government efforts, and overheated criticisms dominated much of the media coverage and commentary. There were diplomatic bright spots as well. In Washington, in April 2004, the Office of the U.S. Global AIDS Coordinator (OGAC) joined UNAIDS, the Global Fund, and Britain in the launch of "The Three Ones," a commitment prompted by demands from overtaxed recipient governments, that donors work collaboratively with them to agree upon one national plan, one coordinating mechanism, and one monitoring and evaluation system for each country. Since that moment, follow-up implementation has been slow.

Elements of a Sustainable U.S. Approach

It is still the early days for PEPFAR, and yet much uncertainty hangs over its future sustainability. Several strains are increasingly at play: worsening budget deficits; clashes between secular and religious constituencies, and their respective allies within Congress; outsized expectations especially regarding treatment; uncertainties over the future carrying costs for programs; tensions between PEPFAR and the Global Fund; and pressures for greater transparency in the disclosure of information. All of these strains will intrude as Congress begins consideration in 2006 and 2007 of reauthorizing programs beyond the first five-year period, which ends in FY 2008. A number of key conditions will be essential to a sustained, effective U.S. AIDS policy.

Continued White House Leadership Will Be Essential

Much of the success achieved thus far has rested on the quality, power, and leadership choices made in the early start-up phase. On policy grounds, a critical test will be whether the president makes the case for a balanced approach between bilateral programs and multilateral approaches that forcefully reaffirms the U.S. commitment to doing its fair share to sustain both PEPFAR and the Global Fund. Similarly, a clear statement on prevention, emphasizing a broad balanced approach, is needed. Not far into the future lies the test of what the president will argue before Congress as the U.S. vision beyond FY 2008. Beyond 2008 lies the challenge of guaranteeing that the next U.S. president attaches equal importance to HIV/AIDS and builds that priority explicitly into his or her foreign policy agenda.

For Prevention

The administration must make it explicit that prevention is indeed a genuine top priority, backed by funding, strategy, and pronouncements. Twenty percent of aggregate resources is simply too little for effective prevention efforts. Standards and prevention targets need better definition, and the official strategy needs to be broadened beyond "ABC," as PEPFAR has begun to do, to encompass a comprehensive approach that addresses the different routes of transmission (including alcohol and injection drug use) and underlying issues such as gender inequity.

Reaching Beyond HIV/AIDS

Part of the forward vision of U.S. HIV/AIDS programs has to be increasingly linking them to the creation of enduring health systems in African countries. African governments will not be able to sustain, politically as well as financially, health systems that address the HIV/AIDS pandemic, as vital as this is, if they are unable to address the health needs of the majority of the population that is facing other major health challenges. The United States has already broadened its focus to TB and malaria. The United States also has a history of assistance in child survival. The next step must be for the United States to reach agreement with African governments and other donors on the investments in facilities, skills, and other inputs that will enable African countries to build and sustain broadly based public and private health systems. Another objective should be to develop viable international schemes to offset the drain of medical talent out of Africa by offering new training and retention programs.

Program Management

PEPFAR, or whatever successor program develops in future years, will need to expand its own staff of skilled personnel. Embassies and USAID missions in several African countries are already straining to develop the sophisticated and technical programs that HIV/AIDS treatment and prevention demand. Short- and long-term assistance to those missions will continue to be a significant demand on OGAC's resources. There also should be a closer coordination, and perhaps an ultimate merging, of OGAC and the Department of State's Office of International Health.

OGAC will also need a strong diplomatic team to leverage higher commitments from other donors, manage relations with host governments, and integrate policy initiatives with the Global Fund, UNAIDS, and others. Likewise the Department of State will need to create professional incentives and the structure necessary to mainstream global health within U.S. foreign policy through, for instance, a global health career track.

Conflict Resolution and Peacekeeping

Conflicts in Africa have taken a terrible toll on the people of the continent. They also threaten the United States. Conflicts have become a breeding ground for international criminal activity, terrorist infiltration, and the spread of disease. They are unsettling the oil-rich Niger Delta region, where stolen oil is traded for arms and politicians are being caught up in a web of crises, crime, and corruption. Similar things are happening in the DRC. African leaders are undertaking impressive initiatives to bring these conflicts under control. But without international cooperation at every level—diplomatic, peacekeeping, and post-conflict reconstruction—African initiatives will fail and so too will many of the U.S. hopes and objectives for the continent.

Conflict's Toll

Conflicts not only undermine stability, they are also a major obstacle to Africa's hopes for economic growth. They are the enemy of environmental conservation, the rights of women, and the protection of children. It is in conflict situations that the worst and most vicious violations of human rights take place. With the Rwandan genocide, the horrific brutalities in the Sierra Leone civil war, the periodic massacres in the DRC, and the genocidal acts and war crimes, including widespread rape, in Darfur, Africa has witnessed and suffered from the worst forms of human behavior. Wars have caused more deaths in Africa than disease and famine. Currently, more than thirteen million are internally displaced persons and more than three million are refugees. In the DRC's civil war, lasting almost a decade now, nearly four million people have died, the vast majority not from direct conflict but from being displaced, by warring parties, from sources of food, medicine, and shelter.

The number of wars in Africa has declined sharply in recent years. Those in the Horn, Sudan (save for in Darfur), Angola, Mozambique, Liberia, Sierra Leone, and Burundi have been ended. Those settlements are testimony to the determination of African and other governments, the UN, and the work of African and international statespersons, who all put great effort into bringing them to a close. Nevertheless, conflict management, mediation, peacekeeping, and post-conflict reconstruction must be higher priorities within U.S.-Africa policy since current conflicts continue in the DRC, Ivory Coast, and Darfur; the settlement between Khartoum and southern Sudan is precarious; and the situations in Liberia, Sierra Leone, Guinea, Togo, Central African Republic, and other weak African states remain threatening.

The U.S. Stake

The humanitarian toll is the most troubling result of conflict and it demands a strong response. Conflict situations, however, also provide an opening for organized crime syndicates, illegal arms merchants, drug dealers, and environmental spoilers. Some of these criminal organizations, in West and Central Africa in particular, are suspected of having links to al-Qaeda. Through illegal trade in diamonds and other precious gems as well as from arms sales, both criminal and terrorist organizations have profited in these lawless environments. Conflicts also divide U.S. allies in the war against terrorism. The 1998 war between Ethiopia and Eritrea interrupted U.S. plans for counterterrorism and peacekeeping training programs in the region. Both countries border the failed state of Somalia, the site of growing terrorist activity.

Conflict situations also make tremendous demands on assistance programs. The United States spent $1 billion on relief following the Rwandan genocide and as much in the wake of the civil war in Sierra

Leone. Hundreds of millions of dollars are being allocated to meet the needs of the more than two million people displaced in Darfur and in neighboring Chad. Much of the U.S. annual $1 billion refugee budget goes to Africa. The UN peacekeeping budget has climbed to where the U.S. share is $1.3 billion, and 75 percent of UN peacekeepers are deployed in Africa.

Why So Much Conflict?

Some of this conflict is rooted in the history of colonial rule and the subsequent pattern of African independence that created states with little national identity, homogeneity, or experience with democratic government. Some derives from a history of weak or oppressive African governments in the first decades of independence, which resulted in discrimination against minority, ethnic, or religious groups. Some of the conflict arises, too, from the growing pressure on the land by a steadily growing population, a situation aggravated by environmental degradation. Rwanda, Burundi, and eastern DRC, sites of the most brutal and systematic warfare in the last twenty years, have also become some of the most densely populated rural areas in the world. Early tension between nomadic and farming groups in Darfur, which later exploded into the genocide of the past two years, arose from increased competition for water and grazing land as the Sahara desert extended southward and a long-term drought set in.

The Cold War brought proxy wars to Africa. In the Horn, Russia and the United States traded partners between Ethiopia and Somalia in the 1970s and supported their respective clients in their wars with each other. The long civil war in Angola was furthered by Cuban troops with Russian support on one side, and U.S. and South African support on the other. In the process, the superpowers lent support to some of Africa's most oppressive and corrupt governments. In Somalia, at the end of the Cold War, the state collapsed altogether. Zaire's (now the DRC) long-time autocratic and venal ruler, Mobutu Sese Seko, was sustained by the United States and European donors as a bulwark against communist influence and state fragmentation in Central Africa, and as an ally in helping rebels in Angola. After Mobutu, the country collapsed into civil war.

Rebellions that start as claims for justice and human rights frequently gravitate into wars over control of lucrative resources. In Sierra Leone and the DRC, fighting has often boiled down to competition for little more than control over diamond and gold mines, and for no larger purpose than greed and the acquisition of weapons. Governments, armies, and local politicians have been corrupted in the process. In the Niger Delta region the most militant insurgent groups are now heavily engaged in stealing oil worth $2 billion or more annually, building up their arms, and allying themselves with corrupt politicians to enlarge their take and increase their leverage.

From all these wars, Africa has become awash in arms. Weapons from the civil war in Mozambique helped to support the war in the DRC and to foster a vast growth of criminality in southern Africa. Traditional conflicts between herders and farmers in Uganda, once fought with spears and with limited loss of life, are now fought with AK-47s, which can be bought for as little as $20 and lead to massive deaths. That level of fatalities, in turn, leads to large-scale and sometimes ethnic warfare. Efforts to control the illegal sales of weapons have foundered on weak enforcement in Africa and, due to U.S. opposition, a very limited UN capability. The U.S. position on this matter should be reversed.

African Leadership in Overcoming Conflicts

African leadership is essential. The politics of these conflicts is very much a complex web of internal and regional relationships that Africans are often better able to address. While the conflicts are largely internal, neighboring countries have been drawn into them, sometimes abetting them. This is true of wars in West Africa—where Liberia, Sierra Leone, Ivory Coast, and Guinea were all parties to recent regional conflicts—and in the DRC, where at one time nine African countries were directly involved in its internal war. Sudan's civil war has affected and been affected by Libya, Egypt, Uganda, Chad, Kenya, and Eritrea. African peacekeepers are also sometimes more welcome in Africa, especially early in a crisis. In the case of Darfur, Sudan refused to tolerate any other peacekeepers but Africans.

Africans have responded and taken an increasingly active role to bring conflicts to an end. Africa provided the first peacekeepers in Liberia and Sierra Leone in the 1990s and again in Liberia in 2003, before the UN authorized a UN force. Africans, under the aegis of the ECOWAS, led the negotiations that ended the Liberian civil war. Together with France they provided peacekeepers to the Central African Republic and most recently to Ivory Coast, again ahead of the UN taking action. In 2003, the AU established a Peace and Security Council, a rough approximation of the UN Security Council. Under the auspices of the council, African leaders have taken the lead to negotiate an end to the wars in Darfur, Ivory Coast, and Burundi. The council sent a contingent of African peacekeepers to Burundi as one of its first acts, and has sent close to 7,000 peacekeepers to Darfur with a commitment to increase that force to as many as 13,000 by spring 2006. The AU has proposed creating a standby force consisting of several regionally based brigades across Africa, ready to step in whenever peacekeeping is needed.

Another important development is the growth of grassroots peace efforts and peacebuilding. Women's groups have become much more active in Africa, insisting on a seat at the table when peace agreements are being negotiated. The Mano River Women's Peace Network and similar groups in Rwanda, Sierra Leone, and other countries, provide an important source of support for peace. Religious institutions are playing a similar role. Finally, the role of elders in bringing about dialogue when combatants will not do so and in mobilizing support for peace processes is an often underappreciated resource.

The Need for International Help

But African leaders cannot carry this responsibility alone and they know it. They lack much of the capacity necessary to achieve their objectives. African peacekeeping operations in Burundi, Liberia, Sierra Leone, Ivory Coast, and earlier in the Central African Republic, had eventually to be taken over by the UN, as Africa could not sustain the expense.

Africans have also needed assistance with equipment, communications, and transport. In Darfur, where Africans have provided the total peace-keeping force, their lack of logistical capability and equipment has led to extraordinary delays. Both the EU and NATO, along with bilateral donors including the United States, are playing an enabling role in assisting AU forces to deploy to Darfur. This logistical and technical support aided the AU in strengthening security within several camps of displaced persons, but did not enable the AU to prevent recurrent attacks across the vast territory in which the victims of the Janjaweed have been displaced.

UN Peacekeeping

The UN currently deploys more than 54,000 peacekeepers in eight missions in Africa. The growth of UN peacekeeping operations in Africa is a turnaround from the 1990s and reflects recognition by both the Clinton and Bush administrations, and by bipartisan majorities in Congress, that such a role serves U.S. interests. UN peacekeeping operations were sharply reduced during the mid-1990s, after the disaster in Somalia, which reduced U.S. support, in particular, for such opera-tions, a reaction that contributed to the failure of UN member states to stop the genocide in Rwanda. But, beginning with the deployment to Sierra Leone in 1999, they have grown and steadily expanded their operations.

Africa is now home to the most complex and demanding UN peacekeeping operations. Ceasefires in most of the countries where they are stationed are fragile. In Liberia, Sierra Leone, Ivory Coast, and the DRC, the UN is also struggling to disarm and reintegrate the many young soldiers (a number of whom are child soldiers) who have become a source of mercenary armies throughout the western Africa region. In the DRC, the UN force moved from a more traditional UN "neutrality" to take military action against rebel militias, thus preserving the prospects for holding elections in the country and bringing, if belatedly, protection to civilians that were suffering from often brutal attacks. The UN force is still insufficient, however, to stop such attacks altogether. On the border between Ethiopia and Eritrea, the UN force is the principal barrier to renewed fighting between two countries engaged in a bitter border dispute. Tens of thousands lost their lives in the previous war. A major UN peacekeeping mission is now deploying to Sudan, where it will play a critical role in protecting the peace between the north and south.

Coalitions of the Willing

On several occasions, short but timely interventions by Western troops prepared to use force have played a critical role in providing initial stability, thereby permitting African and UN peacekeepers to carry out their mission. The United Kingdom sent troops to Sierra Leone to help an initially undermanned UN peacekeeping force protect the capital and push back rebel forces. The EU, together with South Africa, sent troops to eastern DRC to help what was, at the outset, an insufficiently equipped and mandated UN peacekeeping force stop the massacre of civilians by roving rebel forces. France has provided its own troops side by side with African and UN troops in Ivory Coast and Central African Republic. The United States deployed several thousand U.S. marines off the Liberian coast in 2003, sent some on land, and provided important logistical help before an African peacekeeping force could assemble to take charge. This two-step pattern has proved effective in crisis situations where the intervention of combat-capable, well-equipped outside forces may provide the show of force necessary to enable blue-helmeted peacekeepers later to seize and hold the initiative vis-à-vis local militias. History has shown that in most of these cases Western troop presence need only be short-term.

Diplomatic Support

It is not only peacekeeping—and occasionally peace enforcement—where international involvement is essential. None of the major conflicts in Africa can be resolved without both African and international political participation. Leadership by the United States and European countries is necessary to bring the weight of the UN Security Council to bear on a conflict, with the prospect of sanctions and eventual UN peacekeeping operations as necessary. Only Western donors can provide the incentive of post-conflict reconstruction funds. Moreover, in some cases, the parties in the conflict are much more focused on their relationship with the United States than their neighbors. In the case of Sudan, the Khartoum government's interest in improving its relationships with Washington, and having Sudan removed from the U.S. list of states supporting terrorism, was a major incentive in coming to terms with its southern opponents. The United States was influential in getting Rwanda, Uganda, and the DRC to create a trilateral commission to monitor the unstable and contested eastern region of DRC.

U.S. Programs

There is a potpourri of U.S. programs supporting conflict resolution, peacekeeping, and post-conflict reconstruction in Africa, with a clear upward trend. However, funding is sporadic, heavily dependent upon supplemental appropriations, and more responsive to immediate crises than longer-term capacity building. Diplomatic leadership for conflict resolution has been relatively strong in the case of Sudan but limited elsewhere on the continent.

Conflict Prevention and Resolution

The principal ingredient in conflict resolution and mediation efforts is strong diplomatic leadership backed up by dedicated staff and the use of as many elements of leverage as possible. One example was the use of Anthony Lake as a special envoy from the United States to help bring about an end to the 1999 war between Ethiopia and Eritrea. He was a key member of an international mediation effort backed by strong support from the Clinton administration. The United States provided such leadership again in helping bring an end to the north-south civil war in Sudan. A presidential envoy, John Danforth, was appointed early in President George W. Bush's first term. He was backed up by a strong team in the Department of State. Sudan's desire to come out from under U.S. listing as a state supporter of terrorism and to gain economic support for reconstruction gave the United States leverage that it used liberally. The diplomatic effort drew further support from active American constituencies, particularly the evangelical community and the Black Caucus in Congress. The United States also worked closely with the lead African negotiator, Kenya, the African regional body, the Intergovernmental Authority on Development, and a number of European powers.

The United States has not mounted anything as strong to address the other conflicts in Africa. Staff limitations, other policy priorities, and lack of the same pressure from the American public are all factors. Yet the war in the DRC has taken more lives than any other of these conflicts and has ramifications all across Central and southern Africa. The situation in West Africa, Guinea and Ivory Coast, and both Liberia and Sierra Leone threatens a region that is becoming ever more important in energy supplies. The ongoing insurgency and criminal activity in the oil-rich Niger Delta threaten the future of oil supplies from Africa's principal oil producer and indeed the stability of Nigeria itself. And in Sudan, the Darfur situation, which the United States has labeled genocide, continues out of control. Yet there is no longer a presidential envoy for Sudan.

Conflict prevention and resolution should not be an ad hoc activity. Conflict in Africa is still too prevalent and often predictable. The United States needs to dedicate high-level attention to the critical ongoing conflicts in Africa, such as in the DRC, Darfur, Nigeria, and Ethiopia-Eritrea. In some cases presidential envoys are essential, backed up by staff and resources. The United States should also mobilize European attention to these conflicts so that outside attention is coordinated and leadership can be shared. Within the government, the Department of State should create a permanent staff, at both the central and regional bureau level, dedicated to supporting high-level diplomatic activity, monitoring the risks of conflict in Africa, and engaging in conflict prevention, resolution, and post-conflict reconstruction in the situations not receiving higher-level focus.

The Department should further supplement its resources in this area by drawing on the skills and program capabilities in the university, think tank, and NGO communities dedicated to conflict prevention and resolution.[9] These institutions can help both in mediation and

---

[9] Among the many doing this work, the Center for Strategic and International Studies produced an early important study on the post-conflict requirements in Sudan and regularly follows other conflict areas; the International Crisis Group provides regular on-the-ground analyses of conflict situations throughout Africa; the United States Institute of Peace has published

similar efforts, and also, very importantly, in the training of embassy staffs in conflict and risk assessment.

Support for the UN

The United States has supported the growth of UN missions in Africa, but the support has been haphazard, which has inhibited mission effectiveness. The budgeting process needs to be overhauled. The administration budgets for UN peacekeeping in a rigid fashion, requesting funds from Congress only for those missions already approved, even when others are clearly on the drawing board. In FY 2005, the administration needed $680 million in supplemental appropriations to cover UN peacekeeping. For FY 2006, the administration requested $1.036 billion, but acknowledged earlier that it really will need $1.3 billion. That figure did not even include the projected mission in Sudan in 2005, though it may become one of the largest ever. The United States has also resisted, including disarmament, human rights work, and other ancillary peace support programs within the peacekeeping budget, forcing the UN to scramble to raise voluntary contributions for them.

As a result of this budgeting practice, the United States struggles to find funds for new missions as they arise, sometimes urging reduction of the secretary-general's initial recommendation as with Sierra Leone in 1999, insisting on cutting back other UN missions ahead of their time, as the United States did in Angola in 1998, or coming late to the table with approval and funds. In October 2005, the United States helped persuade the UN Security Council to refuse the secretary-general's recommendation to extend the present troop level of the Liberia mission beyond March 2006, and to reject the secretary-general's recommendation to increase the force in the DRC in advance of elections there. Both decisions are shortsighted. These two situations demand long-term UN presence as the countries recover from conflict.

numerous studies identifying the lessons learned in conflict resolution and helps train civil society and NGO personnel in conflict resolution methodology; the Woodrow Wilson International Center has an excellent program on conflict resolution, with particularly effective work in Burundi; the Fund for Peace has a systematic program for identifying the risks of conflict; the Brookings Institution has studied the impact of the AU on the plight of the internally displaced in Darfur; and both the Fund for Peace and the Henry J. Stimson Center have done studies of African peacekeeping capability.

By contrast, NATO forces, including American troops, have remained in Kosovo for six years to assure a peaceful outcome.

If provided additional staff, the UN could provide more support to the AU. For example, the UN could provide support in developing the AU's headquarters capacity with a focus on mission planning and support, coordinating the use of logistics sites, sharing lessons learned and planning expertise, and improving the use of early-warning and analytical information. This was the recommendation of the UN report of the Secretary-General's High-Level Panel on Threats, Challenges, and Change.[10]

Bilateral Support for Peacekeeping

President Bush proposed to the G8 at the Summit in 2004 that the United States and its partners agree to a five-year program to support training and equipment for 75,000 peacekeepers worldwide, with 40,000 of those in Africa. This initiative, the GPOI, which was endorsed by the G8, provides the basis for significant support to the AU's plans for a stand-by force of several regionally based brigades by 2010. In FY 2005, the administration dedicated $100 million for GPOI, most of it from the Department of Defense's budget.

The administration's request for GPOI in FY 2006 is for $114 million, with two-thirds marked for Africa. Congress, however, is moving to cut the total to $100 million. More disturbing, although the administration needs to find $75 million more to cover AU operations in Darfur, there is only $20 million in the African regional peacekeeping budget. This suggests that funding for long-term capacity building in Africa will have to be diverted to Darfur.

It is hard, however, to determine the total amount of support or to develop a coherent strategy for meeting both long-term and more immediate demands. Currently, U.S. support comes from a wide variety of budgets and offices: at least three in the Department of State, several in the Department of Defense, and more from EUCOM and other overseas U.S. commands. The United States already had two training

[10] See *A More Secure Word: Our Shared Responsibility, Report of the Secretary General's High-Level Panel on Threats, Challenges, and Change* (New York: United Nations Department of Public Information, December 2004).

programs under way in Africa before GPOI, the African Contingency Operations Training and Assistance (ACOTA) program and its predecessor the African Crisis Response Initiative (ACRI), which have together trained and equipped 20,000 African peacekeepers since FY 2001; with plans to train 14,000 more in the coming year. Additionally, the United States has provided assistance to African regional peacekeeping operations in Liberia, Sudan, and Sierra Leone through the Peacekeeping Operations account in the Department of State. This same account assists the AU and subregional organizations in their diplomatic and other conflict resolution roles. ACOTA, which replaced ACRI, will presumably be folded into GPOI in FY 2006.

The United States should develop a single overall plan and a single point of coordination for assisting the range of African conflict resolution and peacekeeping capacities. The precedent of funding GPOI from the Defense Department budget is worth preserving. It reinforces the relationship of African conflicts to U.S. security interests and would probably make such funding more assured, but the coordination point should remain with the State Department because of the close relationship to other conflict resolution activities.

Coordination is weak between United States and European training and support activities. This limits interoperability among African forces. Political rivalries among the donors have inhibited efforts to overcome this problem. The introduction of NATO in Africa may offer an important opportunity to help in this area. NATO's decision to provide logistics support to the AU mission in Sudan could open the door to a longer-term relationship with the AU. NATO could also consider a stand-by arrangement to assist Africa peacekeepers to deploy rapidly in future situations. The United States should explore this with both NATO and the AU as GPOI gets further underway. Africa would thus be integrated further into global U.S. security planning.

Democracy and Human Rights

U.S. Interest in Democracy and Human Rights Promotion

The growth of democracy in Africa is one of the most hopeful signs of change on the continent. Democratic African leaders are in the forefront of upholding the principle of constitutional rule, resolving conflict, advocating good governance, and developing sound economic policies. The development of democratic institutions and practices will serve first and foremost the interests of Africans. But partnering with African democracies and giving strong assistance and support to emerging institutions that promote democracy and protect human rights will help in all the areas of U.S. interest in Africa as well. Democratic states will be more stable over the long term, more attuned to the needs of their citizens, share more of America's values, and become better partners to the United States in trade, development, and countering crime and terrorism.

In the 2005 State of the Union Address, President Bush stated, "America will stand with the allies of freedom to support democratic movements in the Middle East and beyond, with the ultimate goal of ending tyranny in our world." Secretary of State Rice cited the spread of democracy as one of the specific outcomes expected from U.S. economic, trade, and peace programs in Africa.

There is already a commitment to democracy from the AU and a positive trend throughout the continent. The United States should continue to encourage this trend through public diplomacy and with incentives in the MCA, debt relief programs, and other instruments. However, U.S. support for democracy, while generally advocated and encouraged, should be strategically focused in countries that carry much influence and reputation in Africa and whose progress on the road to democracy, or steps backward, will have a major impact on the strength of democracy across the continent. Major challenges loom in Nigeria, Ethiopia, Uganda, and Sudan. Success in these countries will be telling for the AU's continuing commitment to democratization. The United States needs also to prepare for a possible collapse or significant unrest in Zimbabwe, which Secretary Rice has specifically condemned for its oppressive political regime. A collapse or widespread unrest would have ripple effects throughout southern Africa.

A Positive, but Fragile Trend

Democracy has taken root in Africa. More than two-thirds of African nations have undergone elections, and the recently established AU has decreed that it will not recognize governments that come to power through unconstitutional means. In response to recent coups in Togo, Guinea-Bissau, and Mauritania, the AU issued forceful condemnations and engineered plans for a return to elected government.

However, African institutions are still fragile. Elections have come faster than the development of responsible and effective political parties, independent electoral systems, fully functioning legislatures, and independent judiciaries. Further, the media are increasingly vibrant, but often poorly funded and subject to bribery and intimidation. Civil society is flourishing as never before, but sometimes lacks the skills or the political support of elites necessary for lasting influence. And some African states remain resistant to democracy, defying both their neighbors and the international community.

Africa has also been the scene of horrific human rights violations. The 1994 genocide in Rwanda, the brutality of civil war in Sierra Leone from 1997 to 1999, and the ongoing rapes and mass atrocities in the DRC and Darfur are testimonies to the challenges still ahead to make Africa safe for all Africans. Such conflicts open a space for exploitation by rapacious criminal and terrorist organizations, further undermining economic development. In addition to the human costs, the United States and other donors pay billions of dollars in emergency and humanitarian aid nearly every year.

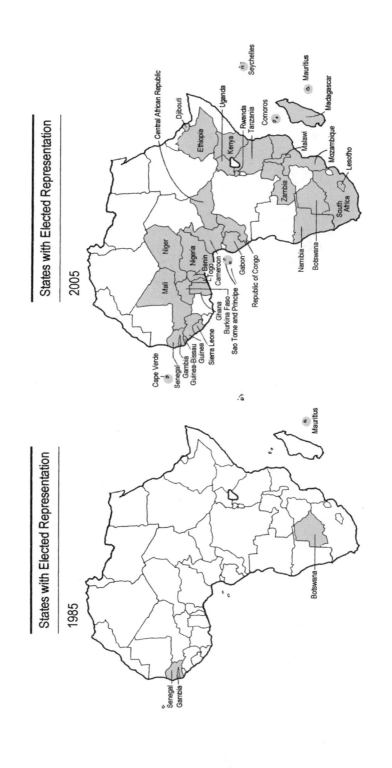

States with Elected Representation

2005

Central African Republic
Djibouti
Uganda
Ethiopia
Kenya
Rwanda
Tanzania
Comoros
Seychelles
Mauritius
Madagascar
Malawi
Mozambique
Lesotho
Zambia
South Africa
Niger
Nigeria
Benin
Togo
Cameroon
Gabon
Republic of Congo
Namibia
Botswana
Mali
Ghana
Burkina Faso
Sao Tome and Principe
Sierra Leone
Guinea
Guinea-Bissau
Gambia
Senegal
Cape Verde

States with Elected Representation

1985

Botswana

Mauritius

Senegal
Gambia

Again on the Ascent: **Ghana Charts a Course for Deepening Democracy**

Decades of authoritarian rule and periodic coups once dimmed Ghana's democratic aspirations. Today, however, Ghana is Africa's most promising democracy. It has carried out successive and transparent elections, and is fastidiously working to put its fiscal house in order.

In a widely peaceful, free, and fair contest, the December 2004 elections returned incumbent President John Kufuor to office. An overwhelming 83.2 percent of the 10.3 million registered voters turned out to vote in this fourth, successive multiparty election since the end of military rule in 1992.

Upon taking office, Kufuor made dealing with the country's substantial external debt, which stood at $6 billion in 2000, a top priority. Against intense domestic opposition, his administration joined the Heavily Indebted Poor Countries Initiative (HIPC), agreeing to implement market-based reforms and invest the savings from debt relief into poverty-alleviation programs. In 2004, Ghana completed the reform process, earning the cancellation of about $2 billion in debt. The government has used debt relief savings to finance development projects, building schools and roads and expanding electricity. And, in June 2005, Ghana was one of eighteen countries selected by the G8 to receive further debt relief—which will wipe out most of its remaining debt.

The Kufuor administration's policies have effectively controlled inflation, which has fallen from 40 percent to 12.5 percent during the past four years, as well as interest and exchange rates. The economy is steadily growing at more than 5 percent. Parliament also has approved new laws to govern public procurement and audits.

Ghana has not solved all of its problems, but it is moving in the right direction. The Kufuor government has a reputation for good governance. Successive and ever more transparent elections, along with a willingness to be evaluated under the African Peer Review Mechanism (a key provision of the New Partnership for Africa's Development) are signs of a rooted democratic culture. As head of ECOWAS, Ghana is also using its democratic clout to contribute to political stability and peace in the region.

Source: "Ghana's Kufuor wins second term, hails 'deepening democracy,' " *Agence France Presse*, December 10, 2004.

Disaggregating Performance

In this realm, as in others, there is not "one Africa." In its *Freedom in the World 2005* survey, Freedom House rated eleven countries in sub-Saharan Africa as free.[11] It rated twenty-one others as partially free. It

[11] See Appendix A in this report.

also classified twenty countries as electoral democracies—each boasting competitive, multiparty political systems, voting by secret ballot, and universal suffrage. The majority of African states are now at what scholars have called the "consolidation stage" of their democratic development. For states, such as South Africa, Botswana, Tanzania, Kenya, Senegal, Benin, Ghana, Mali, Namibia, Malawi, and Zambia, the process of institutionalizing democratic practices is well underway. But countries like Ivory Coast, Sierra Leone, Mauritania, Guinea-Bissau, the DRC, Central African Republic, Rwanda, and Burundi all went from elections to civil war or coups (and in some cases both) and have struggled to get back on the path of democracy.

A number of African countries are also what might be called "pseudo-democracies"—governments that have been elected, but are essentially autocratic. Eritrea, Equatorial Guinea, Gabon, Togo, and Mauritania (under its former president) are examples.

There are serious backsliders too. Zimbabwe stands out as a country that once had great promise and a democratic structure. However, democracy has virtually collapsed after twenty-five years of rule under President Robert Mugabe. Violence, repression, intimidation, disregard for the rule of law, suppression of the media, and continued land seizures have become routine. The economy is near collapse. Leading African states, which have condemned coups and reversed them elsewhere on the continent, have been disappointingly silent on Zimbabwe. Mugabe retains a certain cachet among Africans as a former liberation leader and one who is willing to pull the "lion's [British] tail." Zimbabwe has become the greatest point of contention between Africa and the West on the issue of democracy. It also reveals the limitations on Western leverage and influence if decoupled from African leadership and where there is a willingness to engage bad actors. This situation is, however, now reaching a possible climax that will demand close cooperation between African states and attention by international partners.

Institutional Factors

POLITICAL PARTIES

In many countries, political parties are highly personalized, weak, and lack a solid base of funding. Opposition parties in some countries are highly restricted or even illegal, as in Swaziland. Moreover, where multiparty elections occur, a single party often dominates, despite the abundance of competitors. South Africa has as many as 140 parties and is one of the continent's strongest democracies, yet the African National Congress (ANC) so dominates the political scene that the country has no opposition with a credible chance of winning power. Fortunately, the strength of the courts, the press, and civil society preclude South Africa and the ANC from acting as a one-party state with no checks and balances. Elections in Tanzania and Mozambique in 2004, judged by international observers to be free and fair, have once again returned to power political parties that have ruled since independence.

Party finances also distort the political landscape. A June 2005 study of party finance reform in Africa by the National Democratic Institute for International Affairs (NDI) found that problems stem from "undemocratic, secretive, and unprofessional party organizing practices" that both "undermine public confidence" and "engender governments more susceptible to corruption."

LEGISLATURES AND THE JUDICIARY

African parliaments, in general, are also racked by poor performance. Most parliamentarians lack training and are not supported by competent, professional staff. In Ethiopia, less than a quarter of parliamentarians have a high school education or advanced degrees. Few African countries have independent judiciaries. Lack of confidence in the judicial system and the rule of law not only undermines human rights, but also discourages foreign and local investment.

CIVIL SOCIETY

African civil society, by contrast, has improved dramatically. Civil society has often been the mobilizing force for political change, accountability, and the protest of human rights violations. Today, a rich array of organizations—religion-based, human rights–focused, women's groups, international NGOs, and a host of others—are bringing about changes never experienced in the immediate post-independence decades. Add to this mix a vibrant, if sometimes irresponsible, media and the existence of a growing, engaged, and vocal middle class.

The growth of religious institutions and religious fervor, in particular, is a major phenomenon throughout Africa. The full implications are hard to predict. Especially notable is the growth of independent Christian churches; their banners can be seen in every Nigerian city, and in those of East Africa as well. They seem to provide an escape from the burdens of poverty and loss of confidence in government, and to hold out hope for miraculous cures for diseases like AIDS. Similarly significant are the rise of Protestant evangelical movements (with support from the West, particularly U.S.-based groups), the awakening of mainline Christian churches to social justice and governance issues, and the spread of both radicalized and moderate Islam (with support from Muslim states).

Civil society can play a positive or negative role. Some groups that have sprung up are self-serving, seeking cooperation with autocratic regimes, while others exacerbate religious or ethnic tensions and provoke violence. On the whole, however, the growth of civil society is a positive trend, lending support to democratization, good governance, and peace.

Governance

Good governance—the responsible management of government affairs, services, and finances—is one of the objectives of democratization. Improved governance has become a major criterion for African governments to gain access to new sources of assistance such as the MCA, debt relief, and private investment. Across Africa, many countries are making strides in this area, especially in macroeconomic management. In 2004, the continent experienced an average economic growth rate of 5 percent—an eight-year high. The average fiscal deficit declined to almost zero. Botswana, Mauritius, Mozambique, and South Africa are among the best economic performers and have adopted sound macroeconomic management frameworks and policies.

African governments have made good governance a top priority in their own development agenda. NEPAD established the African Peer Review Mechanism (APRM), which monitors whether participating states' policies and practices accord with agreed political, economic, and corporate governance norms and standards. A total of twenty-three countries have signed up for peer review. Two of the APRM's most innovative features are a self-administered internal review process that each country conducts to determine its own weaknesses, followed by an outside assessment and preparation of a plan for corrective measures. Once complete, a final report is submitted to the participating heads of state and the government.

Major Challenges for the United States

There are several countries of special importance to the United States that are undergoing critical transitions in the next two years. The outcome in these countries could spell success or failure for U.S. hopes and interests in much of Africa.

Nigeria

Nigeria, with 130 million people, is Africa's most populous country. It is also the continent's largest oil producer and a magnet for U.S. private investment. Under President Olusegun Obasanjo, Nigeria has closely allied itself with the United States in the war on terrorism and has been a leader in ending the civil wars in Liberia and Sierra Leone. It has also provided peacekeepers to several conflict situations, including Darfur, and has instituted a significant economic reform program in a country notorious for corruption and mismanagement.

Nigeria has been under military rule for most of its post-colonial history. But in 1999, the military, vastly unpopular after years of corruption and economic decline, yielded to civilian rule. President Obasanjo, himself a former military ruler who was once jailed for his opposition to continuing military rule, was elected president in 1999 and reelected in 2003. The constitution limits a president to two terms. The 2007 election therefore represents a true test of the strength of Nigeria's democratic system, specifically its ability to manage a successful electoral transition, which would be the first in its history.

Unfortunately, the previous two elections were marred by serious irregularities and there have been few systemic improvements since. Nigeria is almost evenly divided between Muslims and Christians, and the political tension within the country as a whole during the coming election is palpable and potentially explosive. President Obasanjo is a born-again Christian. There is suspicion among northern Muslim Nigerians that the president, perhaps with American encouragement (for which there is no evidence), will seek to change the constitution and run again or extend his term.

An election in 2007 that lacks credibility with significant parts of the population, or that is seen as unconstitutional, would spark tremendous unrest. It would jeopardize the economic reforms that President Obasanjo has instituted. There is an urgent need for electoral reform, clarifying rules for presidential succession, and building a strong system of civil society election monitoring. Yet, the United States has cut back sharply on its democratization support funds in Nigeria at this critical juncture.

Ethiopia

Ethiopia is an important partner with the United States in efforts to stem the supply of money, arms, and recruits to terrorist cells along the east coast of Africa and in the Horn. With seventy million people, Ethiopia is also a major country in the fight against HIV/AIDS. Ethiopia remains in a serious border dispute with Eritrea that was the focus of a devastating war in the late 1990s and could potentially turn violent again.

Ethiopia is in the process of a tentative, if stumbling, transition to democracy. Its outcome will significantly affect future stability in the Horn. Recently, Ethiopia conducted its second ever multiparty elections. The opposition parties made significant gains. However, there were charges of major irregularities, including harassment of opposition leaders and party officials, especially in rural areas, unbalanced access to the media, and rigging of ballots. Opposition parties staged demonstrations that turned violent. The EU issued a strongly worded critique of the election that strained its relations with Ethiopia. The United States has been more restrained in its criticism and has urged all sides to remain peaceful as they sort out the situation.

The situation has recently taken an even more negative turn. The Ethiopian government has arrested opposition leaders and charged them with treason. The possibilities for a resolution of the impasse (e.g., the formation of a coalition government, a new general or partial election, or an agreement for the opposition to take its seats in the parliament) now seem less likely. What was at first a promising step toward democracy has turned into the threat of increased military-backed rule and further instability. So far, there is little evidence of concerted international influence on the government. At the same time, Ethiopia and Eritrea are locked in a tense border dispute that could once again break into open warfare.

Sudan

Sudan's success or failure will have more than regional significance. Sudan is roughly half Arab, half African, and largely Muslim, but with a significant Christian population in the south. It is, therefore, an important test of the U.S. goal of bringing democracy to Arab, Muslim populations.

Sudan is emerging from more than twenty years of civil wars between the north and south. The complex peace agreement calls for a major restructuring of the central government to include representation not only from the south but also from opposition parties in the north and, eventually, from previously underrepresented regions of the east and west. Elections are scheduled for 2007. However, the initial assignment of portfolios in the new government does not appear to provide a significant broader role for northern political parties or address the representation of either Darfur or the eastern region. Meanwhile, conflict and major human rights violations continue in the western Darfur region, and there is growing unrest in the east. The death of southern leader John Garang has added to the uncertainty. Extraordinary international attention will be needed to keep the north-south peace process on track and to resolve the ongoing conflict in Darfur.

The United States no longer has a presidential envoy for Sudan. However, Deputy Secretary of State Zoellick is charged with Sudan policy and is dedicating both time and staff to it. Nevertheless, the worsening situation there demands new initiatives, including the replacement or supplementing of the AU peacekeeping forces in Darfur, which are unable to provide sufficient protection for the region's two million internally displaced persons. There is also need for greater pressure on both the Sudanese government and the rebel forces, through independent U.S. and European sanctions or through pressing China and Russia to support UN sanctions.

Uganda

Uganda is an important player in East and Central Africa, and in the Horn. It has been engaged in both conflict and peace processes in the region. It has also received praise from the United States, the UN, and other countries for its successful efforts to combat HIV/AIDS and to overcome a history of misrule, civil war, and mass atrocities. Under President Yoweri Museveni, Uganda has enjoyed increased stability, steady economic growth, and a greatly improved overall human rights situation. President Museveni, who came to power by force, has since been elected more than once. However, he has only in 2005 permitted multiparty elections. Furthermore, if Museveni chooses to continue his presidency for yet another term, after more than twenty years in power, it could indicate a step backward in the development of multiparty democracy, the processes for succession, and strong sustainable democratic institutions. A worst-case scenario sees a post-Museveni Uganda falling back into internal strife.

Zimbabwe

The situation in Zimbabwe, which the secretary of state has rightly singled out as a tyrannical reversal of democracy, may be reaching a climax. Up to now, international criticisms and sanctions have failed to sway the government. African countries have been reluctant until recently to criticize the vaunted liberation leader, Robert Mugabe.

However, the collapsing economy, four million people in need of food aid, the migration to neighboring countries of as many as three million Zimbabweans, and the growing, if divided, internal resistance, all point to a potential collapse of the state or a forced change in leadership. Public criticism of the regime by the U.S. ambassador, in November 2005, added to the tension within the country and placed a public spotlight on the mismanagement of the regime that is causing so much human misery.

The United States needs to prepare for possible state collapse, which would have ripple effects throughout southern Africa. Cooperation with South Africa, which will have a major role in whatever regional responses have to be taken, and a contingency plan for U.S. and other donor assistance to bolster a possible, more responsible successor government should be put into place. It is right to have criticized sharply the Mugabe regime. It is also necessary to avoid the worst possible ramifications of a total collapse, the one thing South Africa has feared the most.

Other Conflict-Ridden Emerging Democracies

Several other African countries are emerging from conflict and are pinning their hopes on elections as the first step toward establishing, or in some cases reestablishing, democracy. Liberia, Ivory Coast, and the DRC are a few examples of such broken places. Establishing democracy in any of these countries will be a major challenge, and the results will be less than perfect. But the alternative could be more war, human rights violations, and the need for outside intervention and emergency aid.

The United States has a special historic relationship with Liberia and has already invested heavily in its reconstruction. The election in December 2005 of Ellen Johnson-Sirleaf as president offers the opportunity to restore both peace and development to this war-torn country. The United States should lead in formulating an international support program for Liberia. The DRC is one of Africa's richest countries in natural resources and its fate impacts on the stability of the whole center of the continent. The United States can look to France and the UN to lead in guiding the peace and reconstruction process in Ivory Coast, and to South Africa with AU support to mediate in Burundi in hopes of avoiding a repeat of the genocide that took place in neighboring Rwanda. But the United States should dedicate high-level attention to the DRC, where as many as four million people have died as a result of the conflict, and continuing conflict threatens the stability of the entire Central Africa region. It is most unfortunate that in October 2005, the United States opposed the UN secretary-general's recommendation to increase the UN peacekeeping operation in the DRC in advance of scheduled elections there.

U.S. Support for Democracy: Matching Rhetoric with Action

The United States has taken several steps to reinforce its support for democracy in Africa. Both the MCA and AGOA include elements of good governance in their qualifying criteria. The United States has insisted on similar criteria for debt relief. Democratization programs are supported by USAID in a number of countries.

Nevertheless, democratization funds for Africa have been cut back, especially funding for the strengthening of institutions that make democracy sustainable after elections. In Nigeria, this aid has been reduced from $20 million in FY 1999 to $3 million in FY 2005. Congress's curtailment of the president's FY 2006 request for the MCA by more than $1 billion also sets back U.S. support for democracy by reducing rewards for African states that are moving in the right direction. MCA funds could be used for a variety of institutional developments that would further encourage democratization. The president's 2006 request for the Transitional Initiative, directed at supporting democratization worldwide, singled out only two African states for attention, Sudan and Ethiopia, leaving out critically important transition countries, such as DRC and Nigeria.

The United States must dedicate more resources to building African institutional support for democracy. The value of negative leverage is in many cases reduced. The United States, the United Kingdom, and the EU have all placed sanctions on Zimbabwe, forced a cutback of multilateral institutions' programs there, and denounced the government's actions, to little effect. On the other hand, UN Secretary-General Kofi Annan's appointment of Anna Tibaijuka, executive director of the United Nations Human Settlements Programme, to investigate the recent destruction of thousands of urban homes and marketplaces by the Zimbabwe government, produced a crack in Africa's indifference. Tibaijuka issued a scathing report that increased outrage within the UN and finally prompted criticism of Zimbabwe from the members of the AU. South Africa, which perhaps has the most leverage in the situation, finally took a tougher line, attaching conditions of both political and economic reform to a loan requested by Zimbabwe. African leadership may be one of the most effective instruments that the United States can engage to further the democratization process in countries falling backwards or resisting the democratic trend.

In Uganda and Ethiopia, the demands on the United States are less for resources than for exerting influence on the processes of democracy. In those cases, however, even where both countries are major recipients of international assistance, negative leverage is limited. The leaders of these countries are strong willed and Ethiopia has already talked of reaching out to China to offset pressures from the EU and the United States on its electoral practices. The United States has not yet, however, assigned high-level diplomats to undertake special efforts with Ethiopia or to mobilize a consortium of countries, both African and others, to address the crisis there. In Uganda, perhaps the best path is for the United States to invest much more in the civil and political institutions that can survive yet another term of Museveni's presidency. In any case, the four countries highlighted deserve special attention if democracy is to flourish on the continent and the recent positive trends are to be sustained. Such a strategy is not yet evident.

U.S. Support for Human Rights: Making "Never Again" a Meaningful Promise

The United States has not hesitated in recent years to speak out on serious violations of human rights in Africa. The secretary of state has singled out Zimbabwe as "an outpost of tyranny" and condemned Sudan for deprivations in Darfur. The Department of State's annual human rights report is an important instrument, helping to focus U.S. leverage and urge African attention to human rights violations wherever they occur. Reports from USAID and from U.S.-based and international NGOs were critical in building support for U.S. leadership in the Darfur crisis. The United States is the only country to label the Darfur situation "genocide," and the United States has been the leading force in seeking strong UN condemnation and sanctions in response to the actions by the government of Sudan and its associated militia.

Despite these steps, Darfur remains in crisis. The AU has not been able to mobilize rapidly or effectively support its current force there, nor is it likely to be able to provide the 13,000-person peacekeeping mission it promised. International assistance to the AU, even through NATO and the EU, has not overcome this problem. The United States must press for the AU to admit its limitations and to ask the UN for further contributions. A rapid mobilization of international force is necessary to protect the displaced and to send a strong message to the Sudanese government. Other steps to further the negotiating process, in particular with the rebel forces, are urgent. Finally, the United States and the EU should be prepared to break the UN logjam on approving sanctions against the Sudanese government, caused by Chinese and Russian objections, by stepping up their own sanctions and confronting China on its role in furthering a humanitarian disaster.

African leadership in human rights will be essential. However, in cases of mass atrocities, as the Darfur crisis shows, Africa must have the assistance and cooperation of the international community. The AU's human rights mechanisms are still not fully in place. AU peacekeepers are already stretched beyond their capacity. These are important areas for U.S. assistance. However, even with assistance to African institutions, none of the steps taken so far by the United States, the UN, or those contemplated in support of African capabilities, ensure that in the event of another Darfur or Rwanda, the international response will be proactive, swift, and effective in preventing mass atrocities—not just reactive after lives are long lost. Such mass atrocities are devastating to every U.S. value and goal. Failure to react in Rwanda was not only a major moral failure, it also damaged the reputation of the United States and the UN in Africa for years afterwards. Further, the repercussions of that genocide are still felt today throughout Central Africa in the instability, fighting, and the episodic massacres that occur in eastern Congo and Burundi. Similarly, the continuing crisis in Darfur now threatens the implementation of the north-south peace process in Sudan in which the United States and others have invested so much. The fighting in Darfur is also spreading into Chad and perhaps farther.

The United States, with its power and its influential position in the UN Security Council, has a special role in strengthening the UN's ability to mobilize an international response to such mass atrocities. The United States should press for strengthening the UN secretary-general's role in identifying the early-warning signs of such atrocities and for recommending swift action by the UN Security Council. Where the Security Council is deadlocked from taking action, the United States should mobilize European and other countries' support for imposing sanction. Finally, the United States should build upon the recent decision of NATO to help the AU to plan for future contingencies for Darfur whereby NATO, the EU, and other countries outside Africa can speed African as well as UN and other international response in a far timelier manner than has been seen in the past.

Investing in Growth

Focusing on Africa's Poverty

Concern over Africa's poverty is at an all-time high. The focus of both G8 leaders and the public in 2005 has been exceptional. This focus is the culmination of years of advocacy for debt relief and aid for Africa by religious groups and other organizations. After sharp declines in aid in the early 1990s, the United States has steadily increased aid to Africa since the mid-1990s. Heartfelt commitments to increase assistance to HIV/AIDS victims and for debt relief have come from a variety of congressional leaders including Jesse Helms, Bill Frist, John Kerry, Russ Feingold, Ed Royce, and the Congressional Black Caucus. As valuable as this response has been, most of the increases in assistance have been in emergency aid, rather than the development aid needed for investments in growth. Donor attention has also shifted frequently, preventing the consistency necessary for sustainable development. U.S. trade policies have also worked against aid recipients, inhibiting their ability to reduce their dependence on aid.

The challenge is to do far better. Neither the United States nor Africa can afford another forty years of stagnation and dependency. Addressing Africa's poverty will require a more comprehensive understanding of the obstacles to growth and development, long-term commitment to priority programs and investments, and recognition by the United States that its trade policies create obstacles to African integration into the world economy.

Measurements of Poverty

Africa is poor in both absolute and relative terms, even when compared to other developing regions. The number of poor people—those living on less than $2 per day—is over 300 million and is expected to rise to over 400 million by 2015.

Africa is the only continent in which the number of malnourished people has risen in the last decade rather than declined. Some 34 percent of the population is undernourished—almost double the figure for the rest of the developing world. Malaria and other diseases kill 3,000 children daily, but far more die of hunger. And just over half of Africa's people have access to clean water, compared to 84 percent of the population in South Asia.

Education is a bright spot where Africa has made strides equivalent to other developing regions. Primary enrollment increased by 38 percent between 1990 and 2000. However, forty-seven million school-aged children receive no education, and of those attending, only one in three finishes primary school.

Poverty and stagnation are not uniform. Almost half of sub-Saharan African countries experienced growth rates of 5 percent or more in 2003. Sixteen countries have averaged 4 percent growth or better over the past decade. Mozambique has reduced the number of people living in poverty. Ghana has a per capita income (adjusted for purchasing power parity) nearly triple that of Zambia. Nevertheless, Africa remains the most impoverished region in the world. Even in Ghana, more than 40 percent of the population lives on less than $1 a day. Continent-wide, per capita income has stagnated during the last thirty years.

The Causes of Poverty are Legion

Ecological Factors

Africa is extremely vulnerable to drought and other natural disasters. Periodic droughts, along with massive locust invasions, frequently cause famine in countries such as Ethiopia, Niger, and Malawi. Ten million people in southern Africa will need food assistance in 2005 because of drought, as will millions of Ethiopians. Africa has less arable land than

Asia or Latin America, and far less land under irrigation. Africa's ecology also accounts for some of its greatest health problems. A combination of high temperatures, ample breeding grounds, and, most significantly, a different species of mosquito translates into a malaria transmission rate in Africa nine times that of India.

Landlocked countries, at great distances from the sea, have limited opportunities to participate in the global economy. A recent United Nations Industrial Development Organization (UNIDO) study found that even if people in these countries worked for free, the costs of transporting their goods to the nearest port would still make them uncompetitive in the world market. Jeffrey Sachs has combined several of these factors to compute a "human vulnerability index." Sub-Saharan Africa far exceeds any other region by this measure.

Governance and Conflict

African governments spent the first decades after independence building and maintaining their national political systems within the boundaries drawn—without reference to ethnicity, language, or religion—by colonial powers. The first post-independence era leaders pursued power through state control of assets and often resorted to political oppression. Urban elites were coopted with blanket offers of government employment and people in rural areas were kept in poverty through price and exchange policies that favored cheap, imported food over local production.

Devastating civil wars in Angola and Congo also cost Africa heavily in lives and wealth. There are more than thirteen million internally displaced people in Africa and 3.5 million refugees. Conflict has caused more death and displacement in Africa than famine or flood.

Administrative weakness and pervasive corruption hamper the delivery of basic health services, education programs, and sound fiscal management. Private investment, both foreign and domestic, is still limited in most African countries by the absence of land titling, excessive bureaucratic constraints on starting and operating businesses, and a lack of access to credit. The World Bank found Africa to be the worst region for doing business because of these constraints. Africa receives less than 1 percent of foreign direct investment and most of that goes to its extractive industries.

Corruption is often cited as one of the principal obstacles to African development. Few African countries rank above four on Transparency International's ten-point Corruption Perception Index. One estimate is that the external stock of capital held by Africans overseas could be as much as $700 billion to $800 billion, more than the total foreign assistance to Africa since independence. Most of this probably came from illegal dealings in oil, timber, diamonds, and other natural resources—rather than from aid—but the point is notable nevertheless. Kenya disappointed donors this past year when members of President Kibaki's administration were found to have embezzled or taken bribes amounting to tens of millions of dollars, and the official in charge of anticorruption measures was forced to flee the country in fear for his life. Illegal sales of minerals have been reported in the DRC, Liberia, and Angola. To make matters worse, the AU remains eight votes short of the fifteen needed to ratify its Convention on Preventing and Combating Corruption. The perception of corruption also has a negative effect on public confidence in aid programs in donor countries. One study found that Americans believe as much as 50 percent of aid is siphoned off by corrupt politicians.[12]

But corruption is a two-way street. Neither the United States nor many European countries have ratified the UN Convention to Combat Corruption. Only recently did EU member states agree to discontinue the practice of permitting their companies to deduct foreign bribes as a business expense. Lesotho has indicted two foreign firms for bribery and is investigating a third. Nigeria is investigating a major U.S. firm. A French arms company is at the center of a huge corruption scandal in South Africa. Zambian investigators have initiated three trials for corruption in the United Kingdom. They are also working on illegal assets held in Belgium and fraudulent debt claims from other EU countries. At the 2005 G8 Summit, member states agreed to help track funds embezzled by corrupt African officials and deposited in U.S. or

---

[12] "Americans on Foreign Aid and World Hunger: A Study on U.S. Public Attitudes," Program on International Policy Attitudes (PIPA) Survey, February 2001, at http://www.pipa.org/OnlineReports/ForeignAid/ForeignAidFeb01/ForeignAidFeb01rpt.pdf.

European banks. However, to date, U.S. and European officials have been more cooperative with helping in criminal investigations of their nationals or companies than in recovery of illegally obtained assets. Some African investigators have had to sign waivers promising that any information they receive will be used solely for criminal, not civil, cases to recover assets. Corruption will continue to be a major concern of Africans and donors alike and must remain on the G8 agenda.

Positive Change

Many of the political, economic, and conflict trials that Africa has endured are now beginning to be overcome. Most African governments are now elected, and there has been a marked shift toward market economies, trade liberalization, and reduction in price and exchange controls. Major efforts by African leaders, regional and subregional African institutions, and the international community are underway to resolve the remaining conflicts on the continent. NEPAD sets forth a continent-wide agenda for improved governance, sound economic policies, and regional integration.

A new breed of finance officials is at the helm of the macroeconomic reforms taking place in several countries. These officials comprise a growing pool of well-trained professionals who often bring world-class experience from international financial institutions such as the World Bank. The Nigerian Finance Minister Ngozi Okonjo-Iweala (a former World Bank vice president) and the Mozambican Prime Minister Luisa Diogo (formerly the minister for planning and finance, who continues to maintain responsibility for planning and the finance portfolio) fall into this category. Both ministers have been recognized for their skill, integrity, and tremendous dedication to their respective economic reform programs.

In Lesotho, another former World Bank official, Timothy Thahane, is minister of finance and development. He has worked to overcome a history of corruption in one of the country's largest infrastructure projects. Lesotho has recently indicted former Lesotho officials, a South African businessman, and several western multinational corporations, and has obtained convictions in most cases. In Zambia, a special task force has brought fourteen corruption cases against a former president and his senior military, civil servant, and intelligence appointees. The task force anticipates recovering at least $200 million from these and other investigations.

The EITI is another vehicle for promoting accountability. This international initiative, chaired by the United Kingdom and consisting of Western and developing country governments, oil and mineral companies, and NGOs, has established principles for making transparent the earnings, payments, and uses of oil and mineral proceeds. The G8 has backed EITI with a similar initiative. Nigeria has endorsed these principles and established an EITI unit in the government. A complete international audit of the oil sector is under way. The audit will not only shed light on this sector, which has a history of corruption, but will also have specific recommendations for ensuring transparency and formalizing these reforms.

In conjunction with World Bank's financing of some of the pipeline costs, Chad has agreed to the establishment of innovative procedures to promote the transparent use of oil proceeds for the benefit of its people. An international body will monitor the proceeds and approve the expenditures from oil production and the profits from the Chad-Cameroon pipeline. Civil society organizations were instrumental in lobbying for this framework and continue to monitor it closely. This experiment is being closely watched for its efficacy. Recently, there has been concern over the Chadian government's request to direct more of the proceeds to security and other expenses and less to be earmarked for education, health, and other direct benefits to the population. There is also concern with the Chadian president's efforts to secure a third term through a change in the constitution and growing security problems in the country. In the meantime, benefits have been flowing to parts of the population from the early proceeds, but it is too early to evaluate this mechanism as a guideline for the future.

Vodacom Congo—Connecting the People of the Democratic Republic of Congo

The story of Alieu Conteh and Vodacom Congo is fast becoming more familiar to Americans in large measure because of Carol Pineau's film *Africa: Open for Business.*

In the 1990s, even as Congo's civil war roiled, Conteh quietly built a cellular network in the DRC. When foreign manufactures refused to ship a cell phone tower to the Kinshasa airport due to rebel activity, he hired local men to collect scrap metal to make their own tower.

By 2001, Conteh's business attracted the South Africa–based Vodacom, and the two formed a joint venture. Today, Vodacom Congo is thriving and profitable, providing service to 1.1 million cell phone customers, and adding more than 1,000 new ones daily.

Congolese villagers in remote jungle provinces are eager for service. In some instances, they built fifty-foot-high tree houses to catch signals from distant mobile towers. According to Gilbert Nkuli, deputy-managing director of Congo operations for the Vodacom Group, "One man uses it as a public pay phone." Anyone wishing to use his platform phone must pay him for access. Aside from helping to create such new economic opportunities for locals, cell phones have also allowed for the expansion of traditional businesses, as in the case of one fishmonger. Nkuli tells the story of an illiterate woman who lives on the Congo River. In his account, the woman asks customers to call her cell phone to request the catch of the day. As Nkuli explains, since she does not have electricity or a freezer, the woman keeps the fish in the river, tethered live on a string, until a call comes in. With an order, she then retrieves the fish and prepares it for sale.

Africa is the world's fastest-growing cell phone market. Usage increased at an average annual rate of 58 percent from 1999, when there were 7.5 million users, to 76.8 million users in 2004. One in eleven Africans is now a cell phone subscriber. Africans now find themselves more connected than ever before, in part due to the efforts of enterprising locals.

Source: Sharon Lafraniere, "Cell phones Catapult Rural Africa to 21ˢᵗ Century," *New York Times*, August 25, 2005.

Promoting Development: No Silver Bullet

While arguments continue over the components of development, there is a growing consensus that there is no single, silver bullet solution. In 2000, and again at the 2005 UN Summit, the nations of the world agreed to support the UN Millennium Development Goals (MDGs), which aim to halve absolute poverty by 2015. Specific MDGs include obtaining universal primary education, eliminating the gender disparity in primary and secondary education, reducing by two-thirds the child mortality rate, and reducing by three-quarters the maternal mortality rate. When G8 leaders met this year, they recognized that the lack of infrastructure in Africa impedes growth. NEPAD and the G8-Africa Action Plan also place important emphasis on improved governance. Africans and foreign advisers alike agree that spurring private investment is another key component of growth, especially the promotion of small and medium-sized enterprises (SMEs) that can contribute the most to employment. Add to this the critical need to protect Africa's environment from degradation and to develop its weak agricultural sector, and one has a full agenda.

Aid and the Problem of Dependency

In assessing the progress so far toward achieving the MDGs, the UN found sub-Saharan Africa to be the region farthest behind. Spurred by this analysis and by the findings and recommendations of the Commission on Africa, the EU, Japan, and the United States have pledged to double aid to Africa over the next five years. Total aid would increase from $25 billion in 2005 to $50 billion by 2010. The world's leading economies also reached agreement on debt relief for fourteen of Africa's poorest countries.

The focus on increased aid and debt relief is welcome. Problems of absorptive capacity, uneven commitment to sound economic policies, and other factors may slow disbursement. Nevertheless, aid increases will be necessary over time, since the MDGs cannot be achieved at the present levels of assistance. The same is true of other requirements for growth, such as infrastructure. Commitments to substantial increases in aid may also act as a powerful incentive for African governments to build their capacity to utilize such aid expeditiously and effectively.

But what the UN study and the commitments at the G8 Summit do not fully address is how to increase aid levels while simultaneously decreasing Africa's aid dependency in the next decade. Many African countries already receive half or more of their annual budgets from foreign aid. In the 1990s, two-thirds of the education and health services in some countries were covered by aid or carried out by international NGOs. Increased aid may well be essential, but without a concerted effort to promote economic growth, sub-Saharan Africa will not be able to sustain the gains it has made in education and health on its own.

Devising a Development Strategy

This report does not aim to provide a full development strategy. The World Bank, the Commission for Africa, several UN reports, and studies from such institutions as the Center for Global Development provide a great deal of analysis and recommendations in that regard. But there are important steps that the United States must take to ensure that the increases in aid now contemplated and the other initiatives underway to assist Africa do not produce disappointing results.

The Importance of Trade

While other developing regions have increased their share of world trade and diversified their exports, the composition of African exports over the past three decades has remained unchanged. Africa is still largely an exporter of raw materials. Its share of world trade during this same period declined from 6 to 2 percent. The answers to increasing Africa's trading potential are, like other aspects of development, complex. Africa needs to increase subregional integration, increase its rural and inland infrastructure, eliminate obstacles to private investment, develop better credit facilities, and undertake customs reform and other forms of trade facilitation.

Subregional integration is especially critical, and it has been recognized as such by NEPAD's Comprehensive African Agriculture Development Plan. Subregional organizations like the Southern African Development Community (SADC), the Common Market of Eastern and Southern Africa (COMESA), ECOWAS, and other such groupings are working on free trade agreements or similar arrangements among their members. However, many of these organizations have overlapping membership, making agreements extremely difficult to harmonize. There are also competing negotiations underway between these groupings and the EU, which is pursuing its own definition of subregional partners, and between the Southern Africa Customs Union (five members within SADC) and the United States. This is an area where international assistance and better coordination between bilateral, regional, and multilateral trade arrangements could be extremely helpful.

But the United States and the EU have an even bigger role to play by opening up their markets to African exports. Africa enjoys low tariffs or preferential treatment on manufactured goods, but it faces high tariffs, non-tariff barriers, and subsidies in the United State and EU that greatly reduce its agricultural exports. Yet agriculture, which employs two-thirds of Africans, has considerable potential. The EU and the United States spend $350 billion each year on protectionist measures and trade subsidies for their respective farming interests. The World Bank estimates that $270 billion of these support payments are trade-distorting. For some agricultural products, U.S. tariffs are as high as 200 percent. U.S. cotton subsidies, which had a negative impact on some of Africa's poorest farmers, were recently ruled WTO-illegal. The WTO issued a similar ruling against EU sugar subsidies.

While G8 leaders pledged in 2005 to reduce these barriers, they provided no timetable or details. President Bush made an even more dramatic statement at the UN in September 2005: he promised to eliminate all subsidies, tariffs, and other obstacles to agricultural trade if all other countries would do so as well. Being dependent upon action by the EU, Japan, and several other countries with strong trade barriers, the president's commitment is welcome, but it is a long way from the promise of early action.

Not all African producers will benefit from a more open market. Some countries that now enjoy preferential access to the U.S. and European sugar markets stand to lose, and countries that import food would face higher prices. But overall, most experts agree that developing countries would gain considerably from such a trade agreement, especially over time and if accompanied by significant assistance for trade facilitation.

TechnoServe in Mozambique: Partnering for a Promising Future

The cashew nut is once again king in Mozambique.

Before the Mozambican civil war, this southern African nation was the world's largest cashew producer. In 1997, with funding from USAID, TechnoServe embarked on a strategy to rebuild Mozambique's cashew industry. It established small-scale rural processing plants close to rural cashew farmers, equipped those plants with technology to extract premium nuts, and provided farmers and employees with an incentive to produce a quality product. TechnoServe spread its innovative business model by establishing eleven plants around the country and along the way helped to restore growth to a sector that once drove Mozambique's economy.

While 95 percent of Africa's annual cashew production must still be exported for processing, TechnoServe's overhaul of Mozambique's cashew industry allows the country to add value through local processing. The cashew sector now generates cash income that supports approximately 940,000 small-scale farmers and their families. The eleven new plants have created jobs for rural people, benefiting an estimated 243,700 rural people (based on an average of five people per family).

Over the years, conditions ripened for direct trade of Mozambique's processed cashews to U.S. consumers. In June 2005, Mozambique's President Armando Guebuza announced the first export sale of "Zambique," his country's newly branded cashew nut, to an American buyer, Suntree.

The revitalization of the cashew sector underlines the benefits that targeted U.S. foreign assistance programs can have on public-private partnerships in Africa. As Lloyd Pierson, the USAID assistant administrator for Africa, noted, "Partnerships between USAID and organizations like TechnoServe help transform good ideas into good businesses which create opportunity and hope." The Zambique brand and its expansion to the U.S. market offer a successful SME model for surmounting the challenges of rural poverty and expanding the range of African products available to American consumers.

Source: "TechnoServe and the Cashew Industry," at http://www.technoserve.org/africa/mozam-cashew.htm/.

Agricultural exports, especially value-added exports, can provide a boost to rural families' incomes, as in the case of Mozambican cashew farmers. Moreover, with a firm timetable for the reduction of trade barriers, African governments and donors could concentrate on the investments that will be necessary to take advantage of multilateral liberalization.

> *A trade agreement in Hong Kong would provide the spur for investment and economic growth that promises a lasting exit from poverty for millions, even billions, of people in developing countries.*
> —Paul D. Wolfowitz, President of the World Bank

An agreement on agricultural barriers has become the major obstacle to an overall agreement in the current Doha trade round. African nations and other developing countries in the WTO have made agreement on agriculture a condition for accepting proposals advocated by the United States and Europe. The latter proposals are for increased market access for U.S. and European financial and other service industries, open access to government procurement contracts, and the worldwide reduction of tariff and other barriers to U.S. and EU exports. The United States has thus a broader interest than African development in seeing the agricultural issue addressed.

The time has come for a determined strategy to open up agricultural trade. The EU and the United States should provide a specific timetable for reduction of these barriers. The president and supportive members of Congress will need to explain to the American public the benefits to the United States from an overall agreement on trade in the Doha round. For example, the relationship to U.S. interests in Africa should also be highlighted, such as the prospect for reducing Africa's dependency on aid and the impact of U.S. cotton subsidies on African farmers in exactly those states where terrorist recruitment is underway. The president and Congress should at the same time begin working on alternative means to protect basic incomes of American farmers and to support a vigorous, market-based agricultural sector.

Improving the Effectiveness of Assistance

The Bush administration has already put in place important new vehicles for assistance. The Millennium Challenge Account is a promising initiative that pledges a sizeable aid package over several years to countries that are performing well. The MCA has approved only a few programs to date (in Madagascar, $130 million over four years), and the amounts do not appear to depart from more traditional levels of assistance. The slow rate of disbursements has led Congress to cut back sharply on the president's request for this program in 2006.

Another challenge is to distinguish more clearly between assistance that invests in long-term development and emergency assistance. On the eve of the 2005 G8 Summit, President Bush noted that U.S. aid to Africa had tripled since 2000 and that an additional $600 million in aid would be granted in FY 2005.

U.S. multilateral aid to Africa doubled between 2000 and 2004, from $2.05 billion to $4.3 billion. U.S. bilateral aid to Africa tripled from $1.139 billion to $3.195 billion. This is, of course, an impressive upward trend. It continued a trend that began in 1996 when the bilateral level was only $635 million and is a reflection of the bipartisan nature of growing U.S. interest in Africa. President Bush's pledge at Gleneagles to double aid to Africa again by 2010 is predicated on Congress appropriating the full projected level for the MCA (by then at $5 billion annually, with half going to Africa), the full projected increases in assistance to combat HIV/AIDS, and a new malaria initiative of $1.2 billion.

However, the actual figures on U.S. aid deserve closer analysis. In FY 2004, nearly half of U.S. bilateral aid to Africa was emergency assistance (largely food aid). All of the additional $600 million announced for 2005 is emergency aid. Other forms of assistance remained relatively static. Emergency aid is and will remain essential for Africa, as droughts and other natural disasters will continue to occur and require major humanitarian response. The United States has been a leader in such aid and Americans can and should feel proud of their country's contributions. However, the United States must not confuse emergency aid with long-term investments for development. Steady increases in the latter cannot be sacrificed to the sporadic demands for emergency aid. Otherwise the long-term investments will simply lack enough support to come to fruition. Disasters will also continue to occur much farther into the future because the systems of food security, safety nets, and increased productivity—investments that would prevent droughts from turning into the horrific pictures of famine we see too often on television—would not be built.

There also must be long-term consistency in aid commitments. Promising investments by USAID and the World Bank in agriculture in the 1970s and 1980s were sharply reduced in the 1990s to the detriment of Africa's food security. According to a recent UN report, microfinance programs, once touted as a promising means to reach the poorest of the poor with noted success in this regard, have "gone out of fashion." Primary health programs were abandoned in countries like Mali because donors did not recognize the need for long-term subsidies in the least developed countries.

The commitment to Africa's development must be understood to involve at least twenty years of dedicated and consistent investment. Programs should not be predicated, as so often in the past, on unreal expectations of self-sufficiency. Congress must understand that even five-year time frames, while valuable markers for evaluation, are not sufficient to turn around basic education systems or primary health services. Short-term expectations lead to abandoning investments and contribute to a sense of failure. This is especially true of the poorest African countries, which will require substantial aid for decades to come.

Sharing the Responsibility

No single donor can address the full array of investments that must be made to overcome the continent's economic problems beyond what African countries can do for themselves. The need for a coordinated multinational approach is essential. Donors speak of coordination, but there is little progress. Despite many calls for change, countries like Tanzania have had to contend with two thousand individual donor-funded projects, each with its own lengthy paperwork requirements. Many African countries' senior ministers must host individual donor missions at least once a week. If there can be little progress on that front, there should be at least agreement on how the many needed investments can be organized in a coordinated manner.

Donors should agree at a minimum on how to meet the necessary funding for the MDGs, agriculture, infrastructure, trade enhancement, improvements in the investment climate, and other requirements, and in which areas individual donors might take the lead. The World Bank may be in the best position to organize such coordination. World Bank President Wolfowitz has made Africa a top priority. New leadership at the Bank and the heightened attention to Africa make this an opportune moment for the Bank to play such a role. The United States should also support a greatly expanded food and funding emergency reserve within the UN system, to include the World Food Program, UNICEF, and other humanitarian agencies. This would alleviate the crash programs and often too-late emergency responses that take place when famine looms, and which then divert donor attention from long-term development to short-term emergencies.

Areas for Special U.S. Attention

Sharing lead responsibilities among donors will enable the United States to concentrate on areas in which it has the greatest expertise, interest, and history of achievement. The United States has unrealized potential across several sectors that can have significant impact on Africa. In each of these, there is the added benefit of strengthening and revitalizing important American constituencies for Africa: universities, the environment and conservation movement, and business experts.

AGRICULTURAL DEVELOPMENT

A recent report by the International Food Policy Research Institute (IFPRI) laid out a comprehensive program for ending hunger in Africa. The program would include reform of agriculture, trade, and tariff policies; investment in rural infrastructure, education, and social capital; crop, land, water, and input management; agricultural research and extension; and investment in women. Specific recommendations include improving soil fertility management through a combination of local knowledge and research-based options that may include integrated pest management, participatory conservation, and use of plant genetic resources, increasing village production infrastructure through threshing and drying floors and basic village storage facilities, and improving crop breeding and biotechnology through private-public partnerships.

Many of these recommendations were part of USAID programs in the 1970s and 1980s, but were drastically reduced in the 1990s in favor of other priorities and fashions. Between USAID and the World Bank, overall assistance to African agriculture dropped by 90 percent in the 1990s. USAID also reduced the number of its missions in Africa, including in Niger—the site of an international famine relief effort in

2005. Recent funding for agriculture is stagnant. The United States spent $514 million in agricultural development assistance for Africa in 2004, compared to $459 million in 2000. On the other hand, USAID funding for health in Africa increased by 61 percent. The United States, which has such strength in agriculture, should be a leader in this area and should commit to being so as long as is necessary to promote genuine food security in Africa. The IFPRI report provides a solid blueprint for reenergizing this commitment.

Support for agriculture should, moreover, go beyond food security and help to develop Africa's export capacity. Greatly increased investments are needed in regional transportation infrastructure, rural credit markets, and new seed varieties for Africa to take full advantage of opening markets. Many African producers that are unlikely to be competitive on global markets have the potential to become regional exporters with the removal of these barriers. Enhanced infrastructure and the larger markets arising from subregional integration would also foster investment in agriculture and agro-industries. USAID has recently announced plans to increase support to NEPAD's Comprehensive African Agriculture Development Plan. Much of that new support could be directed to increasing regional integration and trade facilitation.

BASIC EDUCATION

This is a sector in which the United States has extensive experience. However, as in other aspects of development, the U.S. priorities have shifted over time from primary education, to technical education, to secondary and tertiary education, and now back to primary education. Funding for global basic education has steadily increased in recent years, from $103 million in FY 2004 to $400 million in FY 2005, but much of the recent increases have been earmarked for the Middle East and south Asia. The president's Africa Education Initiative nevertheless provides a focus for this sector if additional funding could be made available. As the initiative documents point out, basic education, especially girls' education, contributes to economic growth, the prevention of HIV/AIDS, and the protection of AIDS orphans from becoming homeless and even becoming child soldiers.

HIGHER EDUCATION

The United States should also resume some programs in higher education. In the 1980s and afterwards, USAID discontinued long and successful programs that twinned African and American universities. A generation of such contact and skills development has been lost. Universities in Africa, during the latter period, declined from lack of funding, overcrowding, and in some cases conflicts. These are nevertheless the institutions that must build Africa's leaders in every field of politics and development. They are the ones with which the United States can develop contact to understand changing social and religious trends and political developments, and to promote cultural understanding. Fortunately, private American foundations that similarly abandoned this field have returned to it. A consortium of the Ford, Rockefeller, Carnegie, and MacArthur foundations have begun investing again in universities in several African countries—and other foundations have recently agreed to join. In conjunction with U.S. programs in agriculture, health, the environment, and private sector development, the United States should complement the foundation programs with exchange programs, faculty training scholarships, and assistance in research.

SCIENCE AND TECHNOLOGY

Closely related to advancing agricultural production, as well as health, is the need for increased scientific and technological capacity in Africa. Unlike Asia and Latin America, Africa did not have a "green revolution"—it has not experienced a dramatic increase in crop productivity. Africa must make some important decisions on the utilization of genetically modified organisms (GMOs), some of which could dramatically increase agricultural output, improve nutrition, and reduce environmental damage from pesticides. The need is all the greater because the AIDS pandemic is cutting down the number of agricultural workers in Africa, reducing Africa's ability not only to feed itself but also to cope with periodic natural calamities. But Africans are being besieged by pressure groups from Europe and elsewhere trying to persuade them of the dangers of this technology. Africans need the independent capacity to make decisions on the basis of their particular needs. Similarly,

Africans need their own leading scientists to address concerns over the safety of vaccines and other medicines, as with the rumors that interrupted the polio vaccination campaign in Nigeria and have arisen over various AIDS medicines.

The UN developed a program for enhancing science and technology in developing countries in the 1980s, but the United States declined to participate. Now foundations, along with the programs in higher education, are focusing once again on science and technology. The Rockefeller Foundation is supporting African research on GMOs and other agricultural technologies. The Gates Foundation is supporting the National Academies of Sciences (NAS) in a ten-year program to enhance the capacity of African academies of science. The U.S. government should lend strong support to these efforts, through agricultural research support and linkages with research institutes in the United States. Like the NAS program, the U.S. government programs should plan in terms of ten years or more in developing the personnel and institutional capacities that will be needed.

SUPPORT AFRICAN REGIONAL INSTITUTIONS

The Africa Union is building up institutions to promote good governance, human rights, infrastructure, and regional trade. The United States should provide assistance and consultation with the African Parliament, the planned Africa Human Rights Court, NEPAD (especially its Peer Review System), and the several subregional organizations that are tackling trade, health, and other cross-border issues. The United States should also give serious consideration to the proposal in the Commission for Africa for an international mechanism for managing large, regional infrastructural projects in Africa. Such an institution would overcome the scarcity of African managerial capacity for such projects, assure appropriate funding and maintenance planning, reduce the opportunities for corruption, and provide for public-private partnerships that would enhance both infrastructure and investment.

IMPROVING THE INVESTMENT CLIMATE

The United States has had several programs in the past to develop credit facilities, expertise, and opportunities for SMEs. Not all of these have been successful. Promotion of SME has also not been as much of a priority in recent U.S. aid programs, despite its importance in increasing employment and contributing to growth. Such programs demand improved credit facilities, business skills training, management oversight, and, perhaps most important, a loosening of bureaucratic obstacles by African governments. The United States should make a careful evaluation of its earlier programs in this sector and develop new and more effective ones. The United States should also continue, as with the MCA grant to Madagascar, to support African reform of land titling and financial instruments and institutions, as well as legal reform, and other means to improve the opportunity for business development. Support should also be given to plans and programs to improve rural infrastructure, subregional infrastructural connections, and other measures that increase subregional trade. USAID has developed a number of promising public-private partnerships for both social and economic programs. These should be expanded, especially into the areas of infrastructure development and the support for SMEs. The United States should also help develop business and financial education facilities in Africa, and offer more fellowships in advanced financial and business management.

Increasing Foreign Direct Investment

The United States should consider tax incentives for American investment in Africa outside the extractive industries—for example, zero tax on repatriated profits and public-private partnerships in infrastructure development. The United States should also make greater packaged use of EX-IM Bank loans, USTDA feasibility studies, OPIC guarantees and loans, and private sector investment. Controversial as such incentives might be, there is a case for them, given the growing competition from Chinese state-owned companies in Africa and the importance of the continent's development to U.S. security and other interests.

Environment

Rapid environmental degradation significantly threatens Africa's development and has consequences for the United States. Desertification is removing thousands of acres each year from agricultural production and increasing competition for land and resources between nomads and farmers. Conflicts in Darfur, Sudan, and parts of Nigeria derive in part from these pressures. Destruction of forests is opening up sources of deadly diseases like Marburg Hemorrhagic Fever and Ebola. Larger and more toxic dust storms from an expanding Sahara are a mounting pollution and public health threat. Restoring and conserving Africa's environment is therefore an essential priority and brings opportunity with it. As Nobel Prize winner Wangari Maathai has shown, rehabilitating forests can improve water quality, generate employment, and promote civil society. Africa's parks and game reserves support a tourism industry that is an economic mainstay for many countries and an untapped growth source for others.

The United States has initiated important environmental programs in Africa. With strong support from former House Africa Subcommittee Chairman Ed Royce and others, the Bush administration launched the Congo Basin Forest Partnership in 2002. This regional conservation model could usefully be adopted elsewhere in Africa as an approach to managing shared ecosystems and building stronger African capacity in natural resource conservation. On the international level, the United States should work through the G8, the UN, and other international forums to elevate the profile of environmental concerns in Africa. European and Asian companies are heavily engaged in environmentally damaging logging practices and overfishing along the African coasts. A code of conduct, accompanied by an expanded set of donor-funded environmental programs, could have a major impact on this area. This area could garner bipartisan support, as the International Conservation Caucus in the Congress has more than one hundred members drawn from both parties.

GROWTH AND DEMOGRAPHICS: THE IMPORTANCE OF POPULATION PROGRAMS

The percentage of Africans seriously malnourished is the same today as in 1970, but the numbers of affected people are more than twice as high. Population growth in Africa is the highest in the world, putting enormous pressure on the continent's limited resources and fragile ecosystems. Ethiopia, a country with chronic food shortages, has more than seventy million people today. By 2030, it could have 140 million. Niger, where the images of its starving children streamed around the globe mobilizing an international emergency feeding program this year, has more than doubled its population. In 1975, Niger's population stood at 4.8 million people. Today there are 11.5 million people, and by 2015 the population is estimated to reach 18.3 million people. Disease and malnutrition cause massive deaths in Africa, but poverty and the fear of losing children early in life contribute to a growing population. A recent study by the Center for Global Development, echoing many earlier studies, found that declines in fertility correlate with economic growth.

Another disturbing demographic factor is the "youth bulge." By 2015, the UN estimates that 42 percent of sub-Saharan Africa's population will be less than fifteen years old, higher than in any other region of developing countries. This demographic is a major challenge in countries already beset by high unemployment. According to studies by Richard P. Cincotta and Robert Engelman, a high proportion of young adults were most closely associated with a new outbreak of civil conflict.[13] The odds of conflict increase in such countries if coupled with a high level of urbanization and scarce resources, which are characteristics of most sub-Saharan African countries.

Yet population has become a neglected area of U.S. policy, overshadowed by the focus on HIV/AIDS and shunned in part because of religious and political opposition to some family planning programs. Family planning funding has thus stagnated when much more needs to be done. The United States has withdrawn its support entirely from the UN Fund for Population Activities. In recent international conferences, the U.S. delegation has opposed reference to "reproductive health services" as implying support for abortion; and the so-called Mexico City rule, which bars recipients of U.S. family planning funds from advocating, counseling, or performing abortions, has led several health institutions in the developing world to refuse U.S. assistance, thereby cutting back on their own programs.

---

[13] See Richard F. Cincotta et al., *The Security Demographic: Population and Civil Conflict After the Cold War* (Washington, DC: Population Action International, 2003).

The focus must shift back to this issue. There are several ways in which population programs can be enhanced. One is to continue the current emphasis on girls' education. Studies make clear that there is a correlation between added years of girls' education and lowered fertility. Recent initiatives by the Bush administration and by other donors to support education in Africa must be maintained at appropriate levels and kept in place for over a generation. There is also an opportunity to utilize the growing investment in health services associated with the fight against HIV/AIDS to strengthen reproductive health programs and to provide them in conjunction with HIV/AIDS and other health services. This would require a significant change in current U.S. policy. But all the programs the United States supports on food security, employment, empowerment of women, achieving universal primary education, and economic growth may well falter if serious attention is not given once again to population.

Conclusion

It is the Task Force's hope that the readers of this report take away two enduring impressions.

First, Americans must pause and reflect on how Africa has become a region of growing vital importance to U.S. national interests. It is outdated and counterproductive to assume that Africa is simply the object of humanitarian concerns or a charity case. The need for a broader approach exists even while the United States should and does stand ready to answer Africa's urgent humanitarian needs. Nevertheless, steadily in recent years, and with an accelerating pace post-9/11, other newly emergent U.S. stakes in Africa have become apparent: energy, terror, and HIV/AIDS. As these interests have grown in importance, Africa has become a more competitive environment, in particular with China's rapidly escalating engagement and quest for Africa's energy and other natural resources. These new realities challenge our thinking and our policies.

Second, a more comprehensive policy is needed. Such a policy is essential for the United States to operate effectively in the increasingly competitive environment in Africa. A broader policy framework is needed to correct U.S. intelligence and diplomatic weaknesses. Such an approach would bind the diverse and promising recent U.S. initiatives—in counterterrorism, HIV/AIDS, and the reward of good governance and economic reform—that today operate in relative isolation from one another into a coherent, dynamic policy. It would recognize the growing capacity of African leaders and institutions working to improve economic performance and governance, to promote democracy, and to resolve conflicts. Finally, this more comprehensive approach will strengthen the U.S. response to Africa's humanitarian needs, not weaken it. The results will not end poverty in Africa, but they will raise hope within the bounds of realism.

After another ten years, even with the policies and programs recommended in this report, the United States has to expect that several African countries will remain very poor, that health and education will continue to require significant improvements, and that chronic conflicts and internal strife will roil some parts of the continent. Natural calamities like drought will regularly occur, as hurricanes each year hit the southern United States, and outside assistance will be needed to help those most seriously affected. The American legacy of compassion toward Africa will persist, just as the United States' special emergency humanitarian capacities will remain vital to the effectiveness of international responses to Africa's humanitarian needs.

But if the recent trends seen in Africa are supported and carried forward through the next decade, as recommended in this report, there are reasonable odds that we will see many African states on sustained paths of economic growth, greater African participation in the world economy, the strengthening of democratic institutions, and far fewer civil or interstate wars. African peacekeepers will be available and better equipped to address threats to peace, reduce the incidence of violence against civilians and the threat of genocide, and serve as a bulwark of UN peacekeeping throughout the world. Agricultural production will have been strengthened, and there will be fairer access to U.S. and European markets. Food security systems along with more amply funded international emergency reserves will make it less likely that the natural calamities that do occur lead to the examples of famine seen in the past.

African countries will be more effective partners in the fight against terrorism. Economic growth, improvements in education and health, and more accountable government will enable African leaders—political, religious, and civic—to mobilize Africa's deep and abiding religious and cultural traditions in resisting the siren song of extremism. Improved intelligence and security systems will enable African governments to identify terrorist inroads and outside efforts to destabilize their countries.

Africa will grow in vital importance as a reliable supplier for the world's energy needs. If reform efforts build new systems of accountability and transparency, the proceeds will go more toward benefiting the people of those countries and help reduce threats to instability that exist in those regions today. The United States, its allies, and the rising economies of Asia will have opportunities to find common ground in enhancing Africa's sound management of these resources and their availability in a free market system.

Africa is on the path to achieving these reforms. But it cannot move forward alone. Nor can the promises of new aid and debt relief in themselves assure African leaders. The United States, as the largest absolute provider of assistance, can take the lead in bringing about a more rational, long-term approach to international cooperation with Africa. The United States can exert more of a leadership role, through its own actions and by persuasion, to bring down the barriers to African agricultural exports and related trade possibilities in order to put Africa on the path to self-sufficiency. The United States can build on its own recent aid initiatives and its pledges to provide more aid by putting into place effective, long-term assistance programs in the areas of agriculture, health, education, environmental protection, better governance, and facilitation of private investment. The United States can help to establish a coordinated donor approach under World Bank leadership, so that African countries are not overloaded with competing programs and administratively burdensome demands that sap their already limited managerial capacity.

The United States can bring greater coherence to its security assistance in Africa. Recent U.S. initiatives in peacekeeping and antiterrorism are promising. But their future funding levels are uncertain and they operate from a plethora of different government offices and institutions. Political oversight of these programs, arguably the most important flaw, has been weak. Timely, sufficiently funded support to conflict resolution, assistance in crisis situations, and countering terrorism all can be enhanced by an improved system of joint military-diplomatic coordination and political oversight.

To meet these objectives, the United States should organize to bring greater coherence and coordination to its policy toward Africa.

Harnessing and utilizing the vast amount of relevant and available U.S. expertise, both public and private, will require high-level direction and coordination, either within the NSC or by senior officials in the Department of State.

However, the first step in achieving a new, more comprehensive approach toward Africa must come from the president and the leaders of Congress. The American public, which has a growing and more widespread concern with Africa, needs nevertheless to understand that a purely humanitarian response, a tendency more toward charity than partnership, will not achieve the desired results. The president and Congress need to articulate the full breadth of U.S. interests in Africa, which are not only humanitarian but in energy, security, and trade. They must make clear that the problems encountered in Africa will not be solved overnight or necessarily in a decade. But African partners are available for attacking these problems. U.S. and African interests can thus be effectively addressed by a sustained, coherent, broad-based policy and the commitment to providing the necessary opportunities and resources. The foundations of strong support for Africa are already present in the American public. It is bipartisan and comes from a broad spectrum of racial, religious, and civic institutions. It can be mobilized to support a more effective policy.

Once in place, the policies, the programs, and the organizational improvements this report recommends should together enhance our position in Africa, deepen the understanding of our intentions, and increase the hopes for Africa.

Additional or Dissenting Views

I am pleased to be associated with this report. It provides a balanced and insightful treatment of some critical African issues, and it is generally both fair and perceptive in discussing U.S. policies.

In a few places, the report appears to lose touch with reality, as in advocating for the AU to appeal to the UN to legitimize a coalition of the willing to undertake military intervention in Sudan. At a minimum, this avenue requires in-depth analysis of who, in practice, might lead and participate in a nonconsensual external military intervention to sort out the mayhem in Africa's largest state. The international appetite for occupying a large area of this largely Muslim society may be limited.

The report's discussion of the challenge posed by China's dynamic presence in Africa sounds at times wistfully nostalgic for an era when the United States or the West was the only major influence and could pursue its reformist, good governance objectives with a free hand. The report is refreshingly sober in noting that that world, if it ever existed, is gone and we must neither abandon our principles nor imagine that we can reform Africa with economic sanctions.

The report underscores the importance of democracy and governance issues. It fails, however, to recognize the cardinal importance of strengthening African state capacity and institution-building in fields as varied as maritime security, police and prisons, and criminal administrative areas. Weak states need more than democracy promotion.

Chester A. Crocker

131

In looking to a better economic future for Africa and its people, we must begin by unflinchingly stating the obvious: the sub-Sahara region has suffered utterly disastrous economic and social performance in recent decades. The economic tragedy that is post-colonial African history, indeed, arguably constitutes the twentieth century's single greatest developmental failure.

By any number of macroeconomic indictors—per capita income, trade performance, and international debt servicing capacity among them—much of the region has experienced not only stagnation but evident retrogression in the past generation. In more human terms, indicators such as life expectancy at birth and school enrollment or completion rates point to a worsening situation for numerous countries in the contemporary sub-Sahara.

In many ways, modern Africa's socioeconomic experiences constitute a terrible mystery: We are still at a loss to explain why performance should have been almost universally disappointing in a vast expanse encompassing so many different ethnicities, cultures, histories, and polities.

But we will delude ourselves, and defraud Africa's future generations, if we cast this profound and complex mystery as a question of foreign aid flows. If sheer volume of official development assistance were the answer to them, Africa's problems would be solved already: The region, after all, has absorbed the adjusted inflation equivalent of over six Marshall Plans during the course of the post-colonial era.

There is more than a slight chance that economic and social conditions in the sub-Sahara will continue to stagnate—or worsen—well into the coming century. This is the prospect that must capture the attention of persons of goodwill the world over. Such an outcome should be morally unacceptable. Much remains to be done, however, if that prospect is to be averted.

Nicholas Eberstadt

I strongly endorse this report, which paints a compelling picture of Africa's strategic importance and outlines a bold new U.S. policy approach. I believe, however, that environmental concerns merit greater prominence in its findings and recommendations.

Traditionally, Africa's natural resources have been viewed through the prism of the competition to reap the benefits of their exploitation. Today, we must also take a hard look at the consequences of their management.

How Africa uses water, forests, rangelands, wildlife, fisheries, and other resources bears increasingly on its security and development. It influences efforts to tackle global problems like climate change and the spread of pandemic disease. It will determine whether the continent's irreplaceable natural heritage—including animals that have captivated humankind for centuries—endures for future generations.

America has set the standard in demonstrating how sound stewardship of natural resources grows the economy, strengthens democracy, and otherwise benefits society. Now is the time to invest in sharing these lessons with Africa.

Nicholas P. Lapham

The time has come for the world to stop talking about Darfur and Congo so diplomatically and up the ante. The report is right about this but is insufficiently precise and bold in what we should do. In short, the Congo peacekeeping mission should be doubled in size (it is still too little for the size of the country). Additionally, NATO should help the AU in Darfur, with a stated willingness to forcibly protect civilians and use much tougher rules of engagement should the violence not be substantially abated within six months, including a Chapter VII–style enforcement mandate, even if Sudan's government disagrees. Washington should be willing to use U.S. Air Force assets in this effort; they are taxed by the Iraq and Afghanistan operations, but not nearly so overused as the U.S. Army and Marine Corps assets.

Michael E. O'Hanlon

Task Force Members

J. Dennis Bonney served as Vice-Chairman of Chevron Corporation, with responsibility for worldwide oil and gas production, before becoming a business consultant. His thirty-five-year Chevron career was spent mainly in the international sector, including the company's operations in a number of countries in Africa.

Lael Brainard holds the New Century Chair in international economics at the Brookings Institution. Dr. Brainard served under President Bill Clinton as Deputy Assistant to the President for International Economics, Deputy National Economic Adviser, and Deputy Director of the National Economic Council.

Chester A. Crocker* holds the James R. Schlesinger Chair in Strategic Studies in the Edmund A. Walsh School of Foreign Service at Georgetown University. Dr. Crocker served for eight years as Assistant Secretary of State for African Affairs under President Ronald Reagan.

Alex de Waal is a Fellow at the Global Equity Initiative at Harvard University and Director of the London-based organization, Justice Africa. Dr. de Waal is the author of the books, *Islamism and Its Enemies in the Horn of Africa* and *Darfur: A Short History of a Long War*.

Note: Task Force members participate in their individual and not their institutional capacities.
*The individual has endorsed the report and submitted an additional or a dissenting view.

Nicholas Eberstadt* is the Henry Wendt Scholar in Political Economy at the American Enterprise Institute for Public Policy Research. Dr. Eberstadt researches demographics, foreign aid, poverty, infant mortality, health disparities, and economic development.

Richard Furman is the Co-Founder of the World Medical Missions and heads the medical ministry of Samaritan's Purse, which supports medicine throughout the world by providing doctors, surgeons, internists, and supplies to areas without sufficient medical capabilities.

Helene D. Gayle is Director of the HIV, TB, and Reproductive Health Program for the Bill and Melinda Gates Foundation. During her twenty-year career, prior to joining the Gates Foundation, Dr. Gayle served in a variety of positions at the Centers for Disease Control and Prevention and retired as Rear Admiral (Assistant Surgeon General) in the U.S. Public Health Service. She is on the board of the Council on Foreign Relations, a member of the Institute of Medicine, and President of the International AIDS Society.

Victoria K. Holt is a Senior Associate at the Henry L. Stimson Center and is the Co-Director of the Future of Peace Operations program. She coauthored a study of peacekeeping reforms at the UN, analyzing implementation of the recommendations for the 2000 Brahimi Report and offering options for further improving peace operations. Ms. Holt served as a Senior Policy Adviser at the Department of State under President Bill Clinton.

Gregory G. Johnson is a retired Navy Admiral. Admiral Johnson most recently served as Commander, Naval Forces Europe (and Africa), and Commander, Allied Forces Southern Europe. He also served in several high-level policy positions, including Executive Assistant to the Chairman of the Joint Chiefs of Staff from 1990 to 1993, and Senior Military Assistant to the Secretary of Defense from 1997 to 2000.

Richard A. Joseph is the John Evans Professor of Political Science and Director of the Program of African Studies at Northwestern University. Dr. Joseph has devoted his scholarly career to understanding political developments in Africa and directed the Africa Governance Program at the Carter Center between 1988 and 1994. Among his many publications is the book, *State, Conflict, and Democracy in Africa.*

Anthony Lake, Chair of the Task Force, is a Distinguished Professor in the Practice of Diplomacy in the Edmund A. Walsh School of Foreign Service at Georgetown University. Dr. Lake served as National Security Adviser under President Bill Clinton. He is the author of several books, including *Somoza Falling* and *The "Tar Baby" Option: American Policy toward Southern Rhodesia,* and is coauthor of *Our Own Worst Enemy: The Unmasking of American Foreign Policy.*

Nicholas P. Lapham* is President of the African Parks Foundation of America. Mr. Lapham was also Vice President for Policy at Conservation International, Senior Program Officer for environment at the UN Foundation, and Senior Adviser to the White House Climate Change Task Force under President Clinton.

Rick A. Lazio is on the Executive Committee at J. P. Morgan where he directs government relations. Mr. Lazio served as a U.S. Representative (R-NY) for eight years. He was also the President and Chief Executive Officer of the Financial Services Forum, an organization aimed at ensuring the stability of global financial systems.

Princeton N. Lyman, Project Director of the Task Force, is the Ralph Bunche Senior Fellow and Director of Africa Policy Studies at the Council on Foreign Relations. Ambassador Lyman served as U.S. Ambassador to Nigeria and South Africa and as Assistant Secretary of State for International Organization Affairs. He is the author of the book, *Partner to History: The U.S. Role in South Africa's Transition to Democracy.*

J. Stephen Morrison, Project Director of the Task Force, is Director of the CSIS Africa Program. From 1996 through early 2000, Dr. Morrison served on the Secretary of State's Policy Planning staff, where he was responsible for African affairs and global foreign assistance issues. At CSIS, he initiated the Task Force on HIV/AIDS in 2001, has directed a succession of major policy reviews, and has published widely on terrorism, energy, conflict, and HIV/AIDS challenges in Africa. Since 1994, he has been an adjunct professor at the Paul H. Nitze School of Advanced International Studies at the Johns Hopkins University.

Michael E. O'Hanlon* is a Senior Fellow in Foreign Policy Studies at the Brookings Institution, specializing in U.S. defense strategy and budgeting, homeland security, and U.S. foreign policy. Dr. O'Hanlon is also a visiting lecturer at Princeton University's Woodrow Wilson School of Public and International Affairs and coauthor of the book, *The Future of Arms Control.*

Raymond C. Offenheiser is President of Oxfam America. Mr. Offenheiser has been the Ford Foundation Representative in several countries and regions and has directed programs for the Inter-American Foundation in South America. He serves on several advisory boards, including the John F. Kennedy School of Government at Harvard University.

Samantha Power is a Professor of Practice in Public Policy at Harvard's John F. Kennedy School of Government. Her book, *"A Problem from Hell": America and the Age of Genocide*, was awarded the 2003 Pulitzer Prize for general nonfiction and the 2003 National Book Critics Circle Award for general nonfiction.

John H. Ricard serves as a Member of the Administrative Board of the United States Conference of Catholic Bishops and Chair of Catholic Relief Services. Before being installed as the Fourth Bishop of the Diocese of Pensacola-Tallahassee in 1997, Bishop Ricard was Chairman of the Domestic Policy Committee of the United States Conference on Catholic Bishops while Auxiliary Bishop of Baltimore.

Gayle E. Smith is a Senior Fellow at the Center for American Progress, where she continues her near twenty-year career in African affairs. Ms. Smith is an Adviser to the UN Commission on HIV/AIDS and Governance in Africa, and is a Guest Scholar at the Brookings Institution.

She is coauthor of the book, *The Other War: Global Poverty and the Millennium Challenge Account.*

Christine Todd Whitman, Chair of the Task Force, is President of the Whitman Strategy Group. Governor Whitman was appointed Administrator of the Environmental Protection Agency in 2000, a post she held until her retirement in 2003. She was Governor of New Jersey from 1994 to 2001 and is author of the book, *It's My Party, Too: The Battle for the Heart of the GOP and the Future of America.*

Task Force Observers

Helima L. Croft
Council on Foreign Relations

Laurie Garrett
Council on Foreign Relations

Christopher E. Haave
Council on Foreign Relations

William L. Nash
Council on Foreign Relations

Appendix

APPENDIX A

2005 Freedom Rating for Sub-Saharan Africa

COUNTRY	FREEDOM RATING*
Benin	Free
Botswana	Free
Burkina Faso	Partly Free
Burundi	Partly Free
Cape Verde	Free
Comoros	Partly Free
Djibouti	Partly Free
Ethiopia	Partly Free
Gabon	Partly Free
Gambia	Partly Free
Ghana	Free
Guinea-Bissau	Partly Free
Kenya	Partly Free
Lesotho	Free
Liberia	Partly Free
Madagascar	Partly Free

Malawi	Partly Free
Mali	Free
Mauritius	Free
Mozambique	Partly Free
Namibia	Free
Niger	Partly Free
Nigeria	Partly Free
Republic of Congo	Partly Free
São Tomé and Príncipe	Free
Senegal	Free
Seychelles	Partly Free
Sierra Leone	Partly Free
South Africa	Free
Tanzania	Partly Free
Uganda	Partly Free
Zambia	Partly Free

Source: Aili Piano and Arch Puddington (eds), *Freedom in the World 2005: The Annual Survey of Political Rights and Civil Liberties* (Lanham, MD: Rowman & Littlefield Publishers, July 30, 2005). Only sub-Saharan countries rated as free or partly free are listed.

APPENDIX B

References

Ashiagbor, Sefakor. *Party Finance Reform in Africa, Lessons Learned for Four Countries: Ghana, Kenya, Senegal & South Africa*. Washington, DC: National Democratic Institute for International Affairs, 2005.

Bryan, Shari and Denise Baer, eds. *Money in Politics: A Study of Party Financing Practices in 22 Countries*. Washington, DC: National Democratic Institute for International Affairs, 2005.

Cincotta, Richard F., Robert Engleman, and Daniele Anastasion. *The Security Demographic Population and Civil Conflict After the Cold War*. Washington, DC: Population Action International, 2003.

Commission for Africa. *Our Common Interest, Report of the Commission for Africa*. March 2005.

de Waal, Alex, ed. *Islamism and Its Enemies in the Horn of Africa*. Bloomington: Indiana University Press, 2004.

Garrett, Laurie. *HIV and National Security: Where are the Links?* New York: Council on Foreign Relations, 2005.

Heller, Peter. "Pity the Finance Minister," *Issues in Managing a Substantial Scaling Up of Aid Flows*," IMF Working Paper WP/05/180. Washington, DC: IMF, September 2005.

Kansteiner, Walter H. *Rising U.S. Stakes in Africa: Seven Proposals to Strengthen U.S.-Africa Policy, A Report of the African Policy Advisory Panel*. Washington, DC: CSIS, May 2004.

Levine, Ruth and the What Works Working Groups with Molly Kinder. *Millions Saved, Proven Successes in Global Health*. Washington, DC: Center for Global Development, 2004.

Morrison, J. Stephen and David L. Goldwyn. *A Strategic U.S. Approach to Governance and Security in the Gulf of Guinea*. Washington, DC: CSIS, July 1, 2005.

Piano, Aili and Arch Puddington, eds. *Freedom in the World 2005: The Annual Survey of Political Rights and Civil Liberties*. Lanham, MD: Rowman & Littlefield Publishers, July 30, 2005.

Rosegrant, Mark W., et al. "*Looking Ahead: Long-Term Prospects for Africa's Agricultural Development and Food Security*," 2020 Discussion Paper 41. Washington, DC: IFPRI, August 2005.

Sachs, Jeffrey. *The End of Poverty: Economic Possibilities for Our Time*. New York: Penguin Press, 2005.

UN Millennium Project 2005. *Investing in Development: A Practical Plan to Achieve the Millennium Development Goals, Overview*. New York: United Nations Development Programme, 2005.

United Nations. *A More Secure Word: Our Shared Responsibility, A Report of the Secretary-General's High-Level Panel on Threats, Challenges, and Change*. New York: United Nations Department of Public Information, December 2004.

World Bank, Africa Region. "Meeting the Challenge of Africa's Development: A World Bank Group Action Plan." Washington, DC: World Bank, September 7, 2005.

Selected Reports of Independent Task Forces Sponsored by the Council on Foreign Relations

In the Wake of War: Improving U.S. Post-Conflict Capabilities (2005); Samuel R. Berger and Brent Scowcroft, Chairs; William L. Nash, Project Director; Mona K. Sutphen, Deputy Director

In Support of Arab Democracy: Why and How (2005); Madeleine K. Albright and Vin Weber, Chairs; Steven A. Cook, Project Director

Building a North American Community (2005); John P. Manley, Pedro Aspe, and William F. Weld, Chairs; Thomas P. d'Aquino, Andrés Rozental, and Robert A. Pastor, Vice Chairs; Chappel A. Lawson, Project Director; Cosponsored with the Canadian Council of Chief Executives and the Consejo Mexicano de Asuntos Internationales

Iran: Time for a New Approach (2004); Zbigniew Brzezinski and Robert Gates, Chairs; Suzanne Maloney, Project Director

Renewing the Atlantic Partnership (2004); Henry A. Kissinger and Lawrence H. Summers, Chairs; Charles A. Kupchan, Project Director

Nonlethal Weapons and Capabilities (2004); Graham T. Allison and Paul X. Kelley, Chairs; Richard L. Garwin, Project Director

New Priorities in South Asia: U.S. Policy Toward India, Pakistan, and Afghanistan (2003); Frank G.Wisner II, Nicholas Platt, and Marshall M. Bouton, Chairs; Dennis Kux and Mahnaz Ispahani, Project Directors; Cosponsored with the Asia Society

Finding America's Voice: A Strategy for Reinvigorating U.S. Public Diplomacy (2003); Peter G. Peterson, Chair; Jennifer Sieg, Project Director

Emergency Responders:Drastically Underfunded, Dangerously Unprepared (2003); Warren B. Rudman, Chair; Richard A. Clarke, Senior Adviser; Jamie F. Metzl, Project Director

Chinese Military Power (2003); Harold Brown, Chair; Joseph W. Prueher, Vice Chair; Adam Segal, Project Director

Iraq: The Day After (2003); Thomas R. Pickering and James R. Schlesinger, Chairs; Eric P. Schwartz, Project Director

Threats to Democracy (2002); Madeleine K. Albright and Bronislaw Geremek, Chairs; Morton H. Halperin, Project Director; Elizabeth Frawley Bagley, Associate Director

America—Still Unprepared, Still in Danger (2002); Gary Hart and Warren B. Rudman, Chairs; Stephen Flynn, Project Director

Terrorist Financing (2002); Maurice R. Greenberg, Chair; William F. Wechsler and Lee S.Wolosky, Project Directors

Enhancing U.S. Leadership at the United Nations (2002); David Dreier and Lee H. Hamilton, Chairs; Lee Feinstein and Adrian Karatnycky, Project Directors

Testing North Korea: The Next Stage in U.S. and ROK Policy (2001); Morton I. Abramowitz and James T. Laney, Chairs; Robert A. Manning, Project Director

The United States and Southeast Asia: A policy for the New Administration (2001); J. Robert Kerrey, Chair; Robert A. Manning, Project Director

Strategic Energy Policy: Challenges for the 21ˢᵗ Century (2001); Edward L. Morse, Chair; Amy Myers Jaffe, Project Director

State Department Reform (2001); Frank C. Carlucci, Chair; Ian J. Brzezinski, Project Coordinator; Cosponsored with the Center for Strategic and International Studies

U.S.-Cuban Relations in the 21ˢᵗ Century (2001); Bernard W. Aronson and William D. Rogers, Chairs; Julia Sweig and Walter Mead, Project Directors

A Letter to the President and a Memorandum on U.S. Policy Toward Brazil (2001); Stephen Robert, Chair; Kenneth Maxwell, Project Director

Toward Greater Peace and Security in Colombia (2000); Bob Graham and Brent Scowcroft, Chairs; Michael Shifter, Project Director; Cosponsored with the Inter-American Dialogue

---

All publications list are available on the Council on Foreign Relations website at www.cfr.org.
To order hard copies, contact Brookings Institution Press: 800-537-5487.